Politics & Me

The psychosocial construct of political beliefs

Colette Marie

Also written by Colette Marie

Nonfiction

F**k It! Memoirs of an Unconventional Yogi

The Miracle of Plant Medicine and The Practice of Yoga

The Power of Change—Insights from an Unconventional Yogi

Color Blind—The Hidden Truths of a Biracial Identity

Antevasin—A yogic path to self-realization & personal freedom

Politics & Me

The psychosocial construct of political beliefs

Lulu Press, Inc.
3101 Hillsborough St.
Raleigh, North Carolina 27607
www.lulu.com

ISBN: 978-1-300-51514-2

Cover, Book Design and Content by Colette Marie Forman
Photos by Colette Marie Forman

Printed in the United States of America

Lulu Press, Inc.
3101 Hillsborough St.
Raleigh, North Carolina 27607
www.lulu.com

Contents

Opening Thoughts   10

Part One
Political Identity-Crisis   14

Chapter 1
The "Radical Left"   15

Chapter 2
The "Alt Right"   22

Chapter 3
The Democrats.   31

Chapter 4
The Republicans   39

Chapter 5
The New Democrats   48

Chapter 6
The Moderate Republicans   57

Chapter 7
The Centrists   66

Part Two
The Psychosocial Construct   75

Chapter 8
The Horseshoe Theory   76

Chapter 9
Construct of Communism   85

Chapter 10
Construct of Fascism   94

Chapter 11
Construct of Socialism   103

Chapter 12
Construct of Conservatism   112

Chapter 13
Construct of Liberalism   120

Chapter 14
Construct of Corporatism   128

Part Three
Political Myopia   135

Political Science Essays   136

Essay #1   137

Essay #2   142

Essay #3   145

Essay #4   148

Essay #5   151

Essay #6   154

Essay #7   158

Essay #8   162

Closing Thoughts   166

Sources   167

Opening Thoughts

When I turned eighteen, the act of voting was not in my daily realm of existence and life. And I make distinction of "our country" regarding the voting age, because in contrast, in the United Arab Emirates, for example, the legal voting age is twenty-five. In other countries, the voting ages range between age sixteen and twenty. However, the UAE holds the oldest legal voting age. The youngest legal voting ages, of sixteen years, includes countries such as Austria, Cuba, Nicaragua, Ecuador, Scotland, Isle of Man, Ethiopia, and Brazil. In fact, "this age has been criticized by most people due to the fact that youths of this age have not yet gotten into the world of employment, tax remission, and home ownership. Many election decisions are believed to revolve around these three issues. As such it is assumed that those at the age of sixteen are not able to vote knowledgeably based on the leaders' policies. However, other critics have observed low voter turnout for persons aged 18 and above due to the apparent lack of interest in politics. As such they suggest that youths of age sixteen are able to turn up for elections in large numbers. During the independent referendum in Scotland in 2014, the inclusion of the youths aged sixteen and seventeen produced positive results. Most of them who felt inadequate to vote resolved to actively seeking information that enabled them to make informed decisions on the voting day. This informed the decision of Scotland to lower its legal voting age to sixteen from eighteen. However, Austria was the first European nation to lower its voting age in 2011."[1]

---

[1] *Legal Voting Age By Country*– worldatlas.com/articles/legal-voting-age-by-country.html

Whether one is sixteen, eighteen, or twenty-five to vote, I will safely assume that the right to vote may be held in higher regard in most other countries. However, I am not certain that voting is absolutely held in higher regard in other countries. I am not even sure if voting is held in higher regard in our own country, given the fact our voter turnout in the United States is woefully low comparatively speaking. Meaning, our highest voter turnout of 67% occurred in this recent presidential election cycle. In 2016, voter turnout was 60%. On average, our voter turnout since Obama ran for office has been hovered around the sixty-percentile range. Prior to that, voter turnout was much lower. We can both agree that voter turnout is improving, however, we are still falling way behind the mark for an overall voter turnout given that there are more than 330 million people in our country. That means, just a little more than half of the country is actively participating in elections. While the rest of the country is not for one reason or another. And those reasons include minors, convicted felons, undocumented immigrants, and non-voters. And I was one of those non-participating people up until the 2016 election cycle.

Admittedly, I did not vote in the 2008 election. I did not feel nor believe that my vote mattered and that elections were rigged. Moreover, I held to firm conspiratorial thoughts that other more hidden and perhaps nefarious powers behind the curtain were the ones who ultimately controlled the flow of elections. Perhaps that remains a truth at some level. But I can say, and perhaps we can both agree that corporations do heavily weigh in on elections, which has been the case over the past two hundred plus years. Though we all say and argue that we live in a Democracy. I have argued for years that we live in a Corporatocracy not entirely a Democracy. Some people I know in the black community believe that "Amerikkka," as they refer to this country as being, is the land of the white supremacist, a land in which black and brown people will forever remain oppressed at some level, in some form or in some way or another. And perhaps that is a reality for a number of black and brown people, for women, for members of the LGBTQIA community, for immigrants, for the elderly, for lower income individuals, for the homeless, for the sick and dying, for anyone who ultimately is unable to get ahead in life, presumably.

I certainly felt this way for a long time myself. Perhaps those thoughts were reinforced when I voted for Al Gore and Florida fumbled the political football due to "hanging chads" and "pregnant chads" which ultimately determined the outcome of an election that I believed Gore had won. It was during the Florida Supreme Court ruling in favor of Bush that I decided that elections were "rigged" and that I no longer wanted to participate. Though, I had no proof they were "rigged." I had no evidence of such facts. And even after Gore conceded, I still harbored that theory without facts and without any real concrete reason to believe otherwise. End of story. I just didn't care after that. I threw up my hands and said f*ck it. I didn't see the point. Therefore, I did not vote for Obama. And I barely voted for anyone in the 2016 election. I did not vote for Trump or Clinton. I voted for Gary Johnson, the Libertarian candidate because I could not bring myself to choose between Donald or Hillary. In my view, they were both two sides of the same coin. In fact, I could not support the political duopoly which persists in this country and fails to adequately meet the needs of its citizens in my humble opinion. And when Trump won, I didn't have a feeling one way or another about his Presidential win. I didn't feel happy nor sad. I simply didn't care. Is it possible that I represent several people who felt the same way? Surely. I am not alone in my thinking. However, times have changed. I have matured. I have educated myself on political matters. I have swung this way and that way on the political spectrum until I landed in a place that is most fitting. Which I shall share with you all. And it is my hope that we both will learn and grow together as we journey down the rabbit hole of political ideologies, beliefs, and psychosocial constructs.

Part One-

Political Identity-Crisis

"No politician can be revolutionary, because the only revolution is spiritual. No politician can be radical either; the very word "radical" means concerning the roots. The politician only prunes the leaves, he has nothing to do with the roots. Only enlightenment takes you to the roots, only meditation takes you to the roots of the problems."

~ Osho

Chapter 1

The "Radical Left"

Ever since Trump was elected in 2016 the phrase, the "radical left" had been spouted out numerously during press briefings, tweets, Facebook Posts, emails, and other media forms. This phrase picked up more steam, in my opinion during his last year in office. Although, it is possible that this phrase was used just as much throughout his term. The only difference in my view, is that I had begun paying more attention and tuning in. Whereas, in previous times, I had chosen not to. As I mentioned in the opening of this book, I made a deliberate choice to not engage in politics in any form. I did not care to listen to State of the Union addresses, press briefings, political committee hearings, none of it. What changed for me was the obvious emotional distress and anger that some of my yogic colleagues and friends were expressing when Trump was elected. Naturally, I would sit and listen to the crying and harsh words. I remember sitting in a community garden one morning after teaching a yoga class in St. Petersburg, at my yoga studio, with two other yogis discussing the election. I remember one individual feverishly expressing her discontent, anger, and sadness over the fact that Trump was elected. And the other young lady commiserated with her, both expressing their lamentations and anger. They were both triggered that late morning in the garden. I, was sitting there listening. Then the one young lady who began venting her frustrations saw that I was undisturbed and took offense to my emotional non-involvement and asked me if I voted for Trump.

I was a little surprised at two things. The fact that she asked me who I voted for and the way in which she asked me. Now I know this woman. She is a lovely lady. But in that singular moment in time, I became annoyed by her. I thought to myself, how dare she ask me who I voted for and how dare she address me in that tone of voice as if to chastise me or criticize me without knowing anything. It was in that moment that I decided to observe people's reactions to Trump getting elected. Why? Because I was genuinely curious about why there was this emotional and psychological break down. And this experience was not limited to just my immediate circle of friends and yoga students. I saw these sorts of emotional break downs on television, on the news, I witnessed these outbursts in the grocery store, in the streets, in yoga studios even. I thought, holy moly what in the world is wrong with these people? Of course, now I understand why people were very angry. However, at the time I just thought it was not normal behavior, especially the sort of vile words that were coming out of the mouths of those who teach yoga. That is not to say, that yoga teachers are not human beings and don't feel. On the contrary, we help those to process their feelings and emotions through the practice of physical postures, movement, breath, mantra and meditation. Yet, from where I was standing, it seemed as though, the Yogic leader in some of these individuals was not present. What was present were just upset people, wanting to know why he was elected and how did that happen?

There was a psychological, emotional, social, and spiritual split happening at the seams of American Democracy which I began to witness within my immediate circle. Although, some would argue, this split at the seams of American Democracy had been in progress for decades, perhaps even longer than that. Moreover, during the time of Trump's inauguration, it was the first time I have ever heard of the group ANTIFA. And as I watched on CNN, these various people dressed in all black, breaking windows of banks, throwing trash cans in the street and into the windows of businesses, and so forth, I grew upset. I thought to myself, "is this how we handle change? Is this that it has come to?" Some have argued that the actions of these individuals were justified. But were they really? The more I watched the news seeing these various violent outbursts by people who were clearly opposed to Trump's presidency, the more repulsed I became at the behavior. Granted, this behavior was not expressed by ALL people who opposed the outcome. Just a very small number of people reacted in this manner. But a larger swath of people was very vocal about their opposition on social media. Which I understand. But that negative vocalization and social media soap box rants grew more intense with every passing month and year. The negative conversations on yoga mats within yoga studios grew more frequent. It was to the point that I decided that I would begin doing some research and reading about American Politics and the Democrat and Republican parties.

That said, in the summer of 2018 I decided to read the book A People's History of the United States by Howard Zinn, which was illuminating to say the least. I began watching all sorts of documentaries including those by Dinesh D'Souza and Michael Moore. I started watching Fox News and CNN. I started listening to Candace Owens podcasts and other's because I wanted to know how people were coming to their conclusions about American Democracy, the Trump Administration and the "Radical Left." This phrase was like a mantra. So much so that, I had begun to associate this phrase with the entirety of the Democrat Party. The negative association grew when I learned that the Southern and portions of Northern Democrats created a group of people called the Ku Klux Klan to suppress votes, hurt other who associated with black people, who were "negro sympathizers", who empathized with the black people, and who helped black people in ways that were viewed as by the KKK as a threat. When I learned of this information, my political pendulum swung to the right. Of course, I was an Independent registered voter in St. Petersburg, Florida. I remained so when I registered to vote in Pennsylvania. However, I did change my party affiliation to a registered Republican voter. I had no real political identity. I do no political roots. I was reacting to what I was reading and witnessing on television and what I was observing within my own circle of friends, on social media and other in person engagements with others.

Naturally, I did not share this information with other people. Simply because it was nobody's business what my political leanings were. I have since changed my voter registration back to being an Independent. But I still do not believe it is anyone's right to know who I voted for and why. That information is personal, much like any of my health concerns or the health concerns of my family members. In sum, these are not things I feel compelled to announce to the world because that is private personal business. However, I do not have any reservations about sharing my thoughts, feelings and political perspectives that may or may not be well received. Because the purpose of this book is to share ideas. And the first idea that comes to mind regarding what I perceive as a political identity-crisis is discussing the nuances and dangers of the small faction of people on the left, referred to as the "radical left", because like anything else, these are the people that live in the extreme left end of the political spectrum. No different from those of the "alt right", who live in the extreme right end of the political spectrum. However, regarding the "radical left" the radical left is a small faction within the Democrat/ Liberal political spectrum. They are the entirety of the Democrat/Liberal political spectrum. That distinction must be made. Because the "radical left" or "far-left" isn't brand new. This new thought and movement spawned during the 60's. For example, according to the Washington Post article, "A Warning from the '60s Generation", John B Judis states that, "in January 1969, Tom Hayden, a founder of the radical Students for a Democratic Society and a leader of the antiwar movement, came to speak at the University of California at Santa Cruz, on behalf of the SDS chapter where I was a member. At the time, many on the new left thought a revolution was imminent. Major cities had been set ablaze by rioters; gun-toting members of the Black Panther Party had confronted legislators in Sacramento; hundreds of thousands were marching against the Vietnam War; and with Richard Nixon in office — and the war showing no signs of abating — the protests were turning violent." [2]

In sum, the idea of the "radical left" has been a working idea for decades. And what that meant then was social change. The methodology and the ideology, however, are what I question by that smaller faction. Some would argue that "radical left" are communists and that these communists are pushing their communist agenda. I have heard that many times over. But the people who make up this "radical left" do not account for all the people who are a part of the Democrat party. That would be unfair to make that assumption or to suggest that everyone who is a Democrat is a Socialist. That is the most absurd generalization known to man. Similarly, we cannot assume that everyone who is a Republican is a racist, white supremacist, fascist, neo-Nazis. Which, in my view, is egregious. The small faction that is the "Alt Right" or the "Far-Right" do not account for every single member of the Republican party. Anyone who holds to this belief only add to the noise and the distortion of what

---

[2] "A Warning from the '60's Generation", *The Washington Post*: nymag.com/intelligencer/2019/03/michael-kazin-radical-left-future.html

we are all currently experiencing as members of society, as voters, as people who hold to a particular political identity. Yet, those are the political identities I question. Because I have come to learn in my own life experience, that my political identity was inherited. I did not craft one out of awareness.

Chapter 2

The "Alt Right"

Without any kind of awareness of what my political leanings were in the past, I voted according to who everyone else voted in my circle. I thought, "well, I'm black, their black, therefore we must vote Democrat." This was my political ideology and identity if you will. Not a very good reason to vote as a Democrat. I had no understanding of what any political party was when I was in my twenties and thirties. I remained ignorant to these things both unconsciously, and consciously. However, during the 2016 election I began to sharply take notice of my immediate environment with regards to people's attitudes about new management. I began to observe without any emotional input whatsoever, other people's behaviors, moods, and actions. I watched. I listened. I took mental notes. Then later I began reading and digging into things, because I was tired of not knowing what all the fuss was about, about why people were so upset, about why people were acting out on the news, pulling people out of their cars, and beating them because they voted for Donald Trump. People were getting spat on, punched, pushed, chased, and terrorized because they were either wearing a MAGA hat, or shirt, or had bumper sticker on their car or showed support for Trump.

I am sure, that these sorts of actions were mostly isolated. But the news did show a fair amount of these activities. And not right-wing news like Fox News. Left-wing news like CNN, MSNBC, etcetera. And I will dive a bit deeper into those distinctions soon. But circling back, media outlets, and social media both continued airing these inhumane acts being committed against people because they voted a particular way. I found this behavior abhorrent. As a result, I continued leaning to the right with my views at some level. Perhaps that was all by design. Because the truth is, I was disgusted with how some people on the "left" were treating some people on the "right". And I say some, because again, this was not a collective attitude. These were some people, acting out against some people. These actions did not define the entirety of a political party. But it did expose a layer of violence and a layer of hatefulness to me that I did not like, care for, or appreciate. I believed that people could do better.

All of this to be said, when I first heard of the "Alt Right", I did not know what the heck that was. Admittedly, I was ignorant. Remember, I had interest in politics and leanings and groups and remained in my bubble until I opened one eye. I was having a conversation with friend on Facebook as he talked about Qanon and the "fake news" and the "alt-right." He told that essentially there is no such thing as an "alt-right" and that it was made up by the "radical left" to discredit conservatives and the Republican party I suppose. Although, again, I just was not sure what the hell he was talking about. However, I went online to research what the "alt-right" was or is, which is just another brand name for the "far right." And thankfully, we have Wikipedia to help us generally clarify was this faction is on the political spectrum. "The alt-right, an abbreviation of alternative right, is a loosely connected far-right, white nationalist movement. A largely online phenomenon, the alt-right originated in the United States during the early 2010s before establishing a presence in other countries and declining after 2017. The term is ill-defined, having been used in different ways by alt-right members, media commentators, and academics.

In 2010, the American white nationalist Richard B. Spencer launched The Alternative Right webzine. His "alternative right" was influenced by earlier forms of American white nationalism, as well as paleo-conservatism, the Dark Enlightenment, and the Nouvelle Droite. His term was shortened to "alt-right" and popularized by far-right participants of /pol/, the politics board of web forum 4chan. It came to be associated with other white nationalist websites and groups, including Andrew Anglin's Daily Stormer, Brad Griffin's Occidental Dissent, and Matthew Heimbach's Traditionalist Worker Party. Following the 2014 Gamergate controversy, the alt-right made increasing use of trolling and online harassment to raise its profile.

In 2015, it attracted broader attention—particularly through coverage on Steve Bannon's Breitbart News—due to alt-right support for Donald Trump's 2016 presidential campaign. On being elected, Trump disavowed the movement. Attempting to move from a web-based to a street-based movement, Spencer and other alt-rightists organized the August 2017 Unite the Right rally in Charlottesville, Virginia, which faced significant anti-fascist opposition. After this, the movement declined. The alt-right is a biologically racist movement promoting a form of identity politics for European Americans and white people internationally. Anti-egalitarian, it rejects the liberal democratic basis of U.S. governance and opposes both the conservative and liberal wings of the country's political mainstream.

Many of its members seek to replace the U.S. with a white separatist ethno-state. Some alt-rightists seek to make white nationalism socially respectable while others, known as the "1488" scene, adopt openly white supremacist and neo-Nazi stances to shock and provoke. Some alt-rightists are antisemitic, promoting a conspiracy theory that there is a Jewish plot to bring about white genocide, although other alt-rightists view most Jews as members of the white race. Anti-feminist, the alt-right intersects with the men's rights movement and online manosphere. The alt-right distinguished itself from earlier forms of white nationalism through its largely online presence and its heavy use of irony and humor, particularly through the promotion of Internet memes like Pepe the Frog. Individuals aligned with many of the alt-right's ideas but not its white nationalism have been termed "alt-lite". The alt-right's membership is overwhelmingly white and male, attracted to the movement by deteriorating living standards and prospects, anxieties about the social role of white masculinity, and anger at leftist and non-white forms of identity politics such as Black Lives Matter. Alt-right material has contributed to the radicalization of men responsible for various murders and terrorist attacks in the U.S. since 2014. Opposed by socialists, liberals, and conservatives, the alt-right's critics accuse it of promoting white supremacism."[3]

All of this is a lot to drink in but does help to shed some light on what this "alt-right", "alt-lite", "alternative right", "far right", thing is to a fair degree. Though I have not read any books about the subject or have had any in person experience with any members of the "alt-right" in my everyday reality, I cannot say that I know any more about what the "alt-right" is outside of what was just shared to you. However, based on what I have learned and what now know, I can say that my friend was incorrect by stating that the "alt-right" does not exist. Although his theory was that the "alt-right" was construct, a fictitious group created by the "deep state." My friend is a Q supporter and a deeply invested conspiracy theorist. And for many reasons, I understand him. Moreover, he has presented some compelling articles and videos to consider. Admittedly, I did, for about two minutes, begin to see what he was seeing. Eventually, I pulled myself back from the edge of insanity because after a while, I began to realize the signs of being under a spell. I felt as though I was

---

[3] *Alt-Right*-https://en.wikipedia.org/wiki/Alt-right

being hypnotized. In sum, I felt that there was an energetic pull towards something that I did not fully understand at the time. I was drawn in, seduced, if you will, into believing something that others began to believe. And that belief was so strong that I felt this compulsion to believe in the rhetoric as well.

Using social media, I decided to run my own little social science experiment, to see whether people with opposing political views could in fact have an intelligent debate and discuss what their views are without insult, displaced emotions, overreactions and so forth. Turns out, the science experiment was not very successful for many months. Generally speaking, by and large, most people had difficulty communicating with others with opposing views. The insults would start, followed by a meme war, followed by name calling, followed by personal digs, which I found to be deeply troubling. In the beginning, friends, that were social media friends, not actual people I have spent time with, would grow frustrated and become indignant with other people on a thread and eventually with me, to the point where I was "unfriended" because I did not agree with their viewpoint, or found their viewpoint lacking specificity and data to support their position. Interestingly, many people on the left side of the political spectrum lacked adequate data and sources to support their positions and spouted obscenities and profanities to drive home their points, which I also found distasteful and unintelligent. Moreover, those on the right side of the political spectrum more often, than not, supplied sources to review, data to consider, and argued their side with intelligence and dignity. However, there were those few on the right that were seeking to cause discord and unnecessary disagreement and therefore were booted from the page entirely. Similarly, those on the left who were seeking to cause discord and unnecessary disagreement were booted from my page. I could not stomach the devolution of discussion because people, regardless of their political leanings could not hold and intelligent debate about their nuance argument points.

In a nutshell, it took months and months before I was able to curate and moderate political debates. As a result of working to find the middle ground with how to communicate with people from both sides of the political aisle, my ability to communicate with others greatly improved both personally and professionally. I was learning the art of debate and began watching others have debates online to see how it's done. I always found the art of debate fascinating. So much so, that I continued this social science experiment for about twenty-two months before I decided to exit the social media platform all together. Though I lost a few folks along the way, I gain so many more new friends. But what was so interesting is that the people that were sending me friend requests were people who either (a) voted for Trump, (b) were non-voters but thinking about voting for Trump in 2020, or (c) were independent voters who voted for Hilary in 2016 but plan to vote for Trump 2020. I very rarely received a request from someone leaned left. Perhaps that was because it appeared, based on my objective stance during most discussions, that I was a "Trump supporter" or someone who voted for Trump. I heard that often on social media. The assumption, I found to be both disturbing and comical. These people didn't know who I voted for. But that did not stop many of them from assuming.

Over time, I began to realize something new about myself. Something that was not present before 2016. Something that I was not aware of before Trump became President. I was having, what I call, a "Political Awakening." It was like my eyes were opening for the first-time regarding politics, American Government, American History, our legislative processes and so forth. Because of Trump winning the 2016 election, I was waking up to all sorts of interesting politically related things and finally became part of the political conversation. Though I fumbled in the beginning with regards to data, statistical information, facts, and so on, I eventually matured and was able to gather information without dipping into "confirmation bias" research tactics which typically is the case with many people when it comes to arguing a point. Granted finding sources which support a point is good. Similarly, finding sources which oppose one's point is also good. So why is any of this important and have to do with the "alt-right"? It is important to note that when it comes to this small faction of individuals, one cannot assume that everyone who leans to the right or is a Republican or who may have voted for Trump for one reason or another is a "racist", "fascist", "white supremacist." That would not be an arcuate statement to make. Moreover, there would be no difference with someone one the right making a similar assumption thinking that all people on the left are "communists", "socialists", "globalists" seeking to push a socialist, communist agenda, ready to take everyone's guns away, silence them and strip them of their Constitutional Rights. That kind of thinking is dangerous.

In sum, there would be no difference from people on the left believing that people on the right don't care about people, the planet, nature, immigrant children, black and brown people, black and brown communities, public education, public housing, social programs, health care and so forth. Because that kind of thinking is equally dangerous. What these extreme and very polarizing beliefs do is continue to perpetuate more and more division and fear, anxiety, stress, worry, anger, rage, and hate. Nothing about these kinds of ideologies is productive, useful, helpful, or meaningful. But this is where we are in today's time. And COVID 19 only further pushed the envelope on that political division between the Democrat voters and the Republican voters of America in more ways than one.

Chapter 3

The Democrats

Previously I spoke about further political division between Democrat voters and Republican voters, as if to suggest that the division which exists, much like the crack in the Grand Canyon splitting solid land mass into two parts, is nothing new. Many people speak today as if this division was created by Donald Trump. In truth, it was not. There has always been a great divide between both the Democrat Party and the Republican party, due to ideologies which conflicted with one another and were pronounced by someone running for office using issues of concern as their party platform. But this wasn't always the case. And though the Democrat party is the oldest of the two parties being founded in 1828 and the Republican party being founded in 1854, once upon a time, there was only one political party in all the land.

For example, "At the beginning of the 19th century the Democratic-Republicans were largely victorious and dominant. The Federalists, in turn, slowly faded, eventually dissolving. Because the Democratic-Republicans were so popular, the party had no less than four political candidates pitted against each other in the presidential election of 1824. John Quincy Adams won the presidency, in spite of Andrew Jackson winning the popular vote. This sparked a strong political division within the party, which eventually caused the party to split in two: The Democrats and the Whig Party. The Democrats were led by Andrew Jackson. He was against the existence of The Bank of the United States and he largely supported state's rights and minimal government regulation. The Whig Party stood in distinct opposition to Jackson and the Democrats, and supported the national bank. The donkey in the Democratic Party's logo is said to derive from Andrew Jackson's opponents calling him a "jackass". "Jackass" is both another word for a male donkey and nickname that describes an unintelligent or foolish person. Instead of disputing this nickname, Jackson embraced it. It has since become an overall symbol of the Democratic Party in general.

In the mid-nineteenth century, slavery was a widely discussed political issue. The Democratic Party's internal views on this matter differed greatly. Southern Democrats wished for slavery to be expanded and reach into Western parts of the country. Northern Democrats, on the other hand, argued that this issue should be settled on a local level and through popular referendum. Such Democratic infighting eventually led to Abraham Lincoln, who belonged to the Republican Party, winning the presidential election of 1860. This new Republican Party had recently been formed by a group of Whigs, Democrats and other politicians who had broken free from their respective parties in order to form a party based on an anti-slavery platform."[4]

However, the evolution of the Democrat party does not stop there. For instance, "at that time in the U.S., tensions were high between Northern and Southern states, causing the Civil War to break out in 1861, in the immediate aftermath of Lincoln's inauguration. In the Civil War, seven Southern States formed the Confederate States of America and fought for detachment from the United States. However, the Union won the war, and the Confederacy was formally dissolved. The issue of slavery was at the center of political disagreement during the Civil War. This caused Republicans to fight for the abolition of slavery and Lincoln signing the Emancipation Proclamation in 1863. At this point in history, the U.S. South was predominantly Democratic and held conservative, agrarian-oriented, anti-big-business values. These values were

---

[4] *History of the Democratic and Republican Parties,*
http://dk.usembassy.gov/da/youth-education-da/the-american-political-system/history-of-the-democratic-and-republican-parties/

characteristic of the Democratic Party at the time. The majority of Northern voters, on the other hand, were Republican. Many of these fought for civil and voting rights for African American people."[5]

Consequently, "after the war, the Republican Party became more and more oriented towards economic growth, industry, and big business in Northern states, and in the beginning of the 20th century it had reached a general status as a party for the more wealthy classes in society. Many Republicans therefore gained financial success in the prosperous 1920s until the stock market crashed in 1929 initiating the era of the Great Depression. Now, many Americans blamed Republican President Herbert Hoover for the financial damages brought by the crisis. In 1932 the country therefore instead elected Democrat Franklin D. Roosevelt to be president. To get the country back on track, Roosevelt introduced his New Deal.

The New Deal launched a number of progressive government-funded social programs, ensuring social security, improved infrastructure, and minimum wage. This meant that a large number of Southern Democrats whose political views were more traditional and conservative, didn't support Roosevelt's liberal initiatives and joined the Republican Party instead. Roosevelt's progressive, liberal policies play an important role in shifting the party's political agenda to look like the modern Democratic Party as we know it today. And, after Roosevelt died in 1945, the Democrats stayed in power with Harry S. Truman in The White House. He continued to take the Democratic Party in a progressive direction with a pro-civil rights platform and desegregation of military

---

[5] *History of Democratic and Republican Parties*, https://dk.usembassy.gov/da/youth-education-da/the-american-political-system/history-of-the-democratic-and-republican-parties/

forces, thereby gaining support from a large number of African American voters, who had previously supported the Republican Party because of its anti-slavery platform. The Democratic Party largely stayed in power until 1980, when Republican Ronald Reagan was elected as president. Reagan's social conservative politics and emphasis on cutting taxes, preserving family values, and increasing military funding were important steps in defining the modern Republican Party platform."[6]

In sum, "following Reagan's two terms in office, his Vice President, George H. W. Bush was elected as his successor in the White House. Since then, Republicans and Democrats have taken turns in The White House. In 2008, Democrat Barack Obama was elected as the first African American president. One of Obama's most notable political achievements was reforming American health care with the Affordable Care Act, commonly known as Obamacare, which ensured that the large majority of Americans became covered by insurance. After two terms in office, Obama's successor, Republican and well-known business man Donald Trump was elected. He moved into the White House in 2017. Two of the main accomplishments on Trump's agenda was providing tax reliefs and to establishing strong borders in order to reduce the number of undocumented immigrants entering the United States. In 2020, Democrat and previous vice president for Barack Obama Joe Biden was elected as Donald Trump's successor. President Biden now serves as the 46. president of the United States."[7]

---

[6] *History of Democratic and Republican Parties*, https://dk.usembassy.gov/da/youth-education-da/the-american-political-system/history-of-the-democratic-and-republican-parties/
[7] *History of Democratic and Republican Parties*, https://dk.usembassy.gov/da/youth-education-da/the-american-political-system/history-of-the-democratic-and-republican-parties/

One important detail post-Civil War, regarding Southern White Democrat Party members, was the creation of the Ku Klux Klan in 1865 in Pulaski, Tennessee. For example, due to unfavorable conditions in the south with plantations and farms ruined, desperation to regain control was afoot. The conditions were ripe for this six-man crew to launch what grew into something bigger than what some may have expected. For instance, "six young ex-confederates met in a law office in December 1865 to form a secret club that they called the Ku Klux Klan. From that beginning in the little town of Pulaski, Tennessee, their club began to grow. Historians disagree on the intention of the six founders, but it is known that word quickly spread about a new organization whose members met in secret and rode with their faces hidden, who practiced elaborate rituals and initiation ceremonies." [8]

Eventually, this group became political, having ties in the political domain, policing various counties in southern states, committing acts of violence, inhumane treatment of both whites in support of blacks and black people in general as a measure of control and dominance over various territories. The Ku Klux Klan proved to be most useful during the late 1860s helping the south to regain political control. For example, "by the mid-1870s, white Southerners didn't need the Klan as much as before because they had by that time retaken control of most Southern state governments. Klan terror had proven very effective at keeping black voters away from the polls. Some black officeholders were hanged and many more were brutally beaten. White Southern Democrats won elections easily and then passed laws taking away the rights blacks

---

[8] *Ku Klux Klan: A History of Racism*, https://www.splcenter.org/20110228/ku-klux-klan-history
racism?gclid=CjwKCAjw3MSHBhB3EiwAxcaEuziM8wD0gCOMwm4Pq2Qcm
mjgHBTHg9NOEkpibrZw8-TBtrBSLdV3RhoCT78QAvD_BwE

had won during Reconstruction. The result was an official system of segregation which was the law of the land for more than 80 years. This system was called "separate but equal," which was half true — everything was separate, but nothing was equal."[9]

In sum, when some people and or Republican voters talk about the Democrats being the party of the Ku Klux Klan, what they leave out is the fact that not every single Democrat voter be them in the North or the South, black or white, were in support of this small-town secret boy's club which grew into a political strong arm of terror and violence. This clan was a small, nay infinitesimal faction of the Southern Democrats made up of six ex-Confederates who plotted the course of their newly formed organization. Interestingly, some continue to (a) use this detail as a Republican Party platform to sway black Democrat voters to return to the so-called fold of their ancestral Republican roots, or (b) deny this detail suggesting that the formation of the Ku Klux Klan was the invention of the Republican Party, which only suggests that those individuals do not know much about the origins of their own party and have not read many history books in their lifetime. But if we understand that the platform messages did shift over time, perhaps we can agree that the modern-day Democrats are no longer the party of voter suppression using a strong arm such as the KKK to enforce its agenda. However, some or perhaps many Republican voters would argue that the modern-day Democrat Party is the party of socialists, using ANTIFA and Black

---

[9] *Ku Klux Klan: A History of Racism*, https://www.splcenter.org/20110228/ku-klux-klan-history
racism?gclid=CjwKCAjw3MSHBhB3EiwAxcaEuziM8wD0gCOMwm4Pq2Qcm
mjgHBTHg9NOEkpibrZw8-TBtrBSLdV3RhoCT78QAvD_BwE

Lives Matter as the strong arms to enforce their socialist and communist agenda. This is where we are.

Chapter 4
The Republicans

During my social media science experiment, I learned that people who subscribe to the Democrat Party ideology and those who subscribe to the Republican Party ideology, more often than not, refuse to listen to each other's political viewpoints when those viewpoints conflict with their political beliefs. Of course, moderating the discourse between these two groups of people has been extremely fascinating to say the least. In some ways, slightly entertaining. Not that I want to see discord or be party to it but fascinating in the sense that people quickly devolve and lose their sense of critical thinking, objective perspective, and willingness to hear the other completely before offering a counterpoint. I suppose this is where I began to learn the art of moderating micro-debates on Facebook threads in which I initiate, in hopes that people begin to hear one another. As I mentioned in a previous chapter, in the beginning I did fumble a lot and lost a few friends along the way. That was not intentional. However, I quickly learned that the best course of action was to post a comment that I found to be engaging, perhaps even fringe, that others would feel inspired to comment on. One post garnered roughly six hundred comments, which was the most any post received. Moderating the back and forth between various people with opposing views was exhausting. I found myself sucked into this hole for hours on end trying to keep things civil. Because as we can probably agree, civil discourse on many levels has become a lost art. People, sometimes quickly devolve in their thinking and become emotional. Some people are immediately triggered and there is no reasoning with that individual when that happens. What's more, some people feel attacked in a conversation and launch profanities as a self-defense mechanism. In cases such as this, objectivity is also lost.

I share all of this because what I found most interesting during this eighteen-month social experiment was how many more people who subscribed to Republican ideology or who were non-voters leaning right, or centrists leaning right, came to the table with excellent points, counterpoints, sources, and other data to support their positions and did so respectfully, most times. Not all the time. But more times than those who subscribed to Democrat ideology or who were non-voters leaning left, or centrists leaning left. There were some occasions when those who seemed to sit on the left came to the table with great points, counterpoints, sources, and other data to support their positions as well. All of this to be said, I learned a great deal in that time. But because those handful of right of center leaning individuals debated their positions so well, I felt inspired to continue my quest on understanding the Republican Party. I wanted to know its history, its current day platform as well as its past political platform and gain a better understanding of the timeline of the Republican Party, being the party of Abraham Lincoln, arguably one of the greatest presidents this country has ever known to Donald J. Trump being the front man, the spokesperson, the representative, the brand, and the image of the Republican Party.

I can say, given the historical roots of the Republican Party, times were very different then and political ideologies were very different then as well. The Republican Party garnered more support by the black community then, than it does today, simply because it was the party in support of black people and in opposition of slavery. In fact, during the Reconstruction era, there were a handful of black Republican politicians. For instance, "since 1870, when Senator Hiram Revels of Mississippi and Representative Joseph Rainey of South Carolina became the first African Americans to serve in Congress, a total of 173 African

Americans have served as U.S. Representatives, Delegates, or Senators."[10] Whereas, the Democrat Party was the party of the South, of tradition, State's Rights, in support slavery, and with support from northern working-class and immigrant groups. Conversely, the Republican Party, post-Civil War was regarded as the party of the North, with strong business and middle-class support.[11] This party platform shift that several Democrat voters' reference was the beginning of the identity crisis respectively. For example, within contemporary American Party System, "it took Nixon's "southern strategy to give the GOP the votes it needed to end Democratic control of national politics. Nixon appealed to disaffected white southerners, and with the help of the independent candidate and former Alabama governor George Wallace, he sparked the shift of voters that gave the Republican Party a strong position in all the states of the former Confederacy."[12]

Moreover, "during the 1980s, under the leadership of President Ronald Reagan, Republicans added two important groups to their coalition. The first were religious conservatives, who were offended by Democratic support for abortion and gay rights and who felt the Democrats were not protecting traditional cultural and religious values. The second were working-class whites, who were drawn to Reagan's tough approach to foreign policy and his positions against affirmative action. Many Republicans consider Reagan's tenure in office as a "golden era" that saw deregulation of many industries, reduced

[10] *Black Americans in Congress*, https://history.house.gov/Exhibitions-and-Publications/BAIC/Black-Americans-in-Congress/
[11] Ginsberg, Lowi, Weir, Tolbert, Cambell, Spitzer, *We the People*, pp. 213
[12] Ginsberg, Lowi, Weir, Tolbert, Cambell, Spitzer, *We the People*, pp. 215

government intervention in the economy, and strong economic growth."[13]

What's more, "while Republicans build a political base around economic and social conservatives and white southerners, the Democrats appealed strongly to Americans concerned with inequality, abortion rights, gay rights, women's rights, the environment, and other progressive social causes."[14] Interestingly, "the Republican Party today is divided in four ways. Pro-business conservatives are traditional Republicans, generally a relatively affluent group that supports small government and lower corporate taxes but also favor global free trade. Far-right conservatives ten to be social conservatives who are opposed to immigration and U.S involvement in the global economy and institutions like the United Nations. Religious conservatives are primarily driven by their socially conservative values, such as opposition to abortion and gay marriage. Finally, libertarians believe in small government and reduced government regulations and emphasize individual freedom." [15] However, I would like to add a fifth "way" in which the Republican Party is divided. And that fifth way is "Trump Supporters." To review, we have (1) Pro-business conservatives, (2) Far-right or "Alt-Right" conservatives, (3) Social conservatives, (4) Religious conservatives and (5) Trump supporters. And fascinatingly enough, that last faction within the Republican Party was just enough of an edge to win an election, in addition to the Democrat Party being splintered themselves.

---

[13] Ginsberg, Lowi, Weir, Tolbert, Cambell, Spitzer, *We the People*, pp. 216
[14] Ginsberg, Lowi, Weir, Tolbert, Cambell, Spitzer, *We the People*, pp. 216
[15] Ginsberg, Lowi, Weir, Tolbert, Cambell, Spitzer, *We the People*, pp. 217

For example, "the 2016 presidential election also revealed serious divides within the Democrat Party between its liberal wing (whose members supported Bernie Sanders) and traditional Democrats, who supported Hilary Clinton and who tend to be older and hold a mix of moderate and liberal values. Such divisions within the party have contributed to the Democrats losing the White House and Congress in 2016."[16] The fact remains that even though, Clinton won the popular vote by roughly three million votes, which is a slim margin, Trump was the guy that seemed to best represent a margin of people who felt left out of the political fold. And those individuals, the mid-westerner consisting of primarily white farmers, plant workers, and lower income families and individuals, felt as if Trump had their best interests at heart and therefore felt inspired to make their voices be heard by voting for a man whom they felt would increase jobs, where jobs had gone missing, bolster conservative family values in schools, put conservative families first, create jobs, close the border where jobs are perceived to be lost to undocumented workers, reduce foreign relations and focus on what America needs and not on what other countries need. The slogan of "Make America Great Again" was the slogan that spread like wildfire across the entire nation. And Trump was the man, in their eyes, who could make America great again, whatever that meant or means.

There is much debate these days about the identity of the Republican Party as a whole, whether it's the part of traditional Republican Party values and platform or the Party of Donald J. Trump. The term "Trumpism" is now part of Political Science and academia. That man branded himself into academia! That alone is impressive. That

---

[16] Ginsberg, Lowi, Weir, Tolbert, Cambell, Spitzer, *We the People*, pp. 217

said, let us briefly review what Wikipedia has defined as "Trumpism". "Trumpism is a term for the political ideologies, social emotions, style of governance, political movement and set of mechanisms for acquiring and keeping power that are associated with Donald Trump, and his political base. "Trumpists" and "Trumpian" are terms referring to those exhibiting characteristics of Trumpism, whereas political supporters of Donald Trump are known as "Trumpers". The exact terms of what makes up Trumpism are controversial. Though Trumpism is sufficiently complex to overwhelm any single framework of analysis, it has been called an American political variant of the far-right and of the national-populist and neo-nationalist sentiment seen in multiple nations worldwide from the late 2010s to the early 2020s."[17]

I do like how "Trumpism" is referred to as a "political variant", in the description, written by someone or a group of people. "Trumpism" is just another social construct created by someone to try and understand the psychology of those who support Trump as fervently as they do. But the construct has created much fan fair within the Republican Party and in the country, as well as abroad. Trump has become larger than life itself. He has become iconic in a way. And in as much as that description may make you cringe; it is a fact. The Trump brand of politics has made its way to just about every country and to almost every mind of those who either voted for him, who voted against him, who subscribe to his brand of politics within their own governments, who hate him, who fear him, who wish to be in his good graces, who want to be in his camp, who love him, who worship him, and so forth. I do believe that no other president ever has garnered that much support and anti-support. Trump

---

[17] *Trumpsim,* https://en.wikipedia.org/wiki/Trumpism

has become a household name whether some people like it or not. And the Republican Party seemingly wishes to remain in the light of Trumps celebrity and popularism because that's the kind of charm and magic the Republican Party wishes to have and missed since the days of Ronald Reagan. In fact, Ronald Reagan was probably considered in the way at some level and still is in some ways. Some Trump supporters argue that is the best president this country has ever had since Reagan. And in some ways, those individuals are not entirely wrong. If we all agree that Reagan was one of the best presidents, this country has ever had. Which we can more than likely, disagree on that point. Only those who voted for Reagan believe that Reagan was the best president this country ever had next to Abraham Lincoln.

And allow me to say, Reagan is light years away from Lincoln. These two men are not at all the same. They exist on opposite sides of the political spectrum as far as I am concerned. Firstly, Lincoln was a man of the people, all the people, black, brown, male, female, merchant, farmer, military, tradesman, etcetera. Secondly, he sought fairness and equality for all people regardless of where they lived, how much they had, whether their skin was white or black, etcetera. Thirdly, Lincoln was an intellect, an educator, a writer, a lawyer, a public speaker, a politician, and a public servant. He wasn't perfect but he was certainly idealistic enough to inspire positive way of seeing the world at large. Simply put, Lincoln was in a class all by himself. And Reagan was not Lincoln. Nor will he ever be considered as such. However, if we are to compare two men, Reagan and Trump would be more alike than not. However, Reagan did maintain political norms. He conducted himself accordingly and held himself to higher standard. Reagan was not a pompous man, nor was he a narcissistic person who actively sought to stir the political pot whenever the moment presented itself. But he also did not have Twitter and Facebook back then either. And I wonder, what would his presidency have been like if Reagan did have social media at his disposal?

Chapter 5

The New Democrats

Recently, I heard, during an NPR interview pertaining to various party platform issues, the phrase or term, "New Democrats." At the time of my eve's dropping, I thought to myself, "what in the world is a New Democrat?" Moreover, just the night before, I had a dream in which a friend of mine shouted out, in a townhall meeting, that the era of the black moderate is dead. Firstly, I was aware that I was dreaming, and I was baffled by her outburst. But it also got me thinking about what she meant. And what, by definition, is a "black moderate" and why has that era come and gone? Secondly, I was not sure if what she meant was her truth or was gross generalization, as she followed up her claim stating that, people must choose a side. I assume she meant a political side. Her claim and follow up claim, pointed to the idea that people who sit in the middle of the political spectrum must decide about which party to become part of because of where we are right now, politically. I suppose in some respect she is not entirely wrong about her assertions. However, if I, someone who is not entirely certain of either party, must decide on which party to select, would need to continue doing more research into each political platform, because as it stands, I am not a fan of either, neither am I a fan of the political duopoly in which we are all subject to.

All of that being said, let us take a moment and define what a New Democrat is. You may know this information. Or you may not. In either case, having it in plain sight couldn't hurt as having this information present in the moment will prove useful as we continue our political journey into these psychosocial constructs of political beliefs. And for the sake of continuity, let us explore what Wikipedia. For example, "New Democrats, also known as centrist Democrats, Clinton Democrats, or moderate Democrats, are a centrist ideological faction within the Democratic Party in the United States. A New

Democrat is defined as a member of the Democratic Party who advocates or supports centrist or neo-liberal policies. As the Third Way faction of the party, they are seen as culturally liberal on social issues while being moderate or fiscally conservative on economic issues. New Democrats dominated the party from the late-1980s through the mid-2010s."[18]

Circling back to the statement from the dream, "the era of the black moderate is dead.", I can now better understand what was meant by that. For example, the definition of the moderate "is an ideological category which designates a rejection of radical or extreme views, especially in regard to politics and religion. A moderate is considered someone occupying any mainstream position avoiding extreme views and major social change. In United States politics, a moderate is considered someone occupying a centre position on the left–right political spectrum."[19] The key phrase to consider here is "avoiding extreme views and major social change", as it pertains to a black person in this country. When the statement, "the era of the black moderate is dead" was made, "avoidance" is what was being referenced. The avoidance of extreme views and major social change for black people in this country, given where we are socially, economically, historically, as black American's, translates into the realization that the era of sitting on the fence on social change is over. In other words, being complacent is dead and one must choose a side to stand on socially, politically, environmentally, and so forth, whether one is black, white, Asian, Latin x, immigrant,

---

[18] *New Democrats*, https://en.wikipedia.org/wiki/New_Democrats
[19] *Political Moderate*, https://en.wikipedia.org/wiki/Political_moderate

undocumented, male, female, non-gender specific, trans, gay, straight, etcetera.

So, if the age or the era of the black moderate is over, then the black moderate can consider this newer political identity as a New Democrat for example. Being that we live in the age of political identities, which I have branded as psychosocial constructs, a moderate on the left can easily consider this third faction within the Democrat Party. You or I can essentially call ourselves New Democrats if someone asks, if that is the direction our political beliefs point towards. However, when it comes time to voting, if you are a left-leaning centrist, your vote will still go to Democrat candidates, presumably. But you can review each candidate through a new lens. And perhaps through this new lens, your vote may go to some Democrat candidates and some Republican candidates depending on the intentions of each candidate, what they stand for, and how well they best serve communities. Moreover, there are several congressmen and women who have band together to create the New Democrat Coalition, which I found to be fascinating.

Now you may be asking yourself, like I asked myself, what is this coalition about? In sum, "The New Democrat Coalition is made up of 95 forward-thinking Democrats who are committed to pro-economic growth, pro-innovation, and fiscally responsible policies. New Democrats are a solutions oriented coalition seeking to bridge the gap between left and right by challenging outmoded partisan approaches to governing. New Democrats believe the challenges ahead are too great for Members of Congress to refuse to cooperate purely out of partisanship." [20] Moreover, according to Ballotpedia, "The New

---

[20] *About* Us, https://newdemocratcoalition.house.gov/about-us

Democrat Coalition was founded in 1997 and describes itself as a group of "forward-thinking Democrats who are committed to pro-economic growth, pro-innovation, and fiscally responsible policies."[21] What's more, "The NewDem Action Fund is the political action committee of the New Democrat Coalition. The group described its work as helping "elect and re-elect forward-thinking leaders who will help ensure everyone in America has the opportunity to earn a good life."[22]

In essence, there are people that you can elect as Congress people that may be members of this coalition or seek to be a part of this coalition, which may align with your political beliefs and values, as a New Democrat or Moderate Democrat, potentially. Being that it is a distinct third faction within the Democrat Party, focusing your political efforts on those Politian's who subscribe to the New Democrat Party beliefs may be your best option. And I must be clear and state that the New Democrat Party is not the same or has any affiliation with the political philosophy which is Democratic Socialism. In fact, Democratic Socialism is only a political philosophy not a faction within the Democrat Party. Some seem Republican voters to think that, just because some members of Congress such as Alexandria Ocasio-Cortez announced her beliefs and philosophy of Democratic Socialism, that the entire Democrat Party subscribe to the philosophy of Democratic Socialism and further believe that Democrats are all socialists and communists. I think that AOC and Bernie Sanders and others who believe that Democratic Socialism would be the better fit for this country, lost any hope of pushing their agenda when they used the word "socialism." That word is a "trigger" word, so deeply rooted in the mind,

---

[21] *New Democrat Coalition*, https://ballotpedia.org/New_Democrat_Coalition
[22] *New Democrat Coalition*, https://ballotpedia.org/New_Democrat_Coalition

that various older generations are not willing to hear what anyone has to say when the world "socialism" is involved. And it's not just the "Baby Boomers" and the "Silent Generation" that feel this about the construct of "socialism." This trigger word is similarly viewed as something horribly wrong for this country, by Generation X and some Millennials. Generationally speaking, the concept and philosophical construct of Democratic Socialism appeals to the much younger generations, such as Generation Z and Alpha Generation.

Therefore, when Bernie Sanders entered the race back in 2016, he won over many younger people. His ideals of social and economic equality were appealing. He was the political Independent, a Senator from Vermont, kind of a lone wolf if you will, who stepped on stage with some big goals for the country, that I do not think were well received by Republican Voters, or people leaning to the right. All they hear in his speech's is the word "Free." And that word "free" is associated with the trigger word, "socialism" or "socialist." You, see? The psychology of these words plays a significant role in the minds of many people. Conversely, you had Trump and his rhetoric about "Make America Great Again", which seemed to charm a number of potential voters, and Republican voters. In fact, whoever managed his marketing and branding, did a stellar job. Honestly, whoever those people are did what no other president was ever able to do and that was to use social media, news media, hashtags, slogans, colors, apparel, mass marketing campaigns, text messages, and other means to get their message across all platforms. And it worked out brilliantly. Because I do not believe these ideas came from his brain. I believe a team of people worked feverishly to help create the "45" brand, the "MAGA" brand, "Donald J. Trump for President" brand.

And his rhetoric of making America great again, were also trigger words, especially for those older generations, coming back to that. And to also, those mid-west farmers, middle America, the mill worker, the plant worker, the steel worker, the members of society who have seen their farms go up in smoke, who have lost their land, who have lost their jobs because they went overseas, who have watched the world become more diverse than they care to admit, and who have witness more people coming in from other countries, allegedly "taking" their jobs, and so forth. These are the people that felt comforted by hearing the words, "Make America Great Again" and the promises of getting jobs back, building a border wall and unsubscribing to various foreign policies which allegedly do not benefit this country. These words, from a entertainment personality, who knows how to work the cameras, say all the right things, behave in a way that may be perceived as strong, masculine, tough, and able to stand up to other world leaders like a "man", rang true for a number of people who either leaned right, or were already Republican voters.

Even I got swept up by them. Even I was charmed. Even I was feeling a particular way that I have never felt before. I was feeling, what only can be described as electrified for two seconds. Meaning, Trump brought his narcissism and his ego, his charm, his ambitions to every person in every event, and debate on and off camera. As I mentioned before, I was waking up to the political process and conversation. Due to this man's inherent need to stay relevant in an ever-changing society, he pushed his way through, reaching millions of households and minds of American people. And I happened to be one of those people he pushed his way through to reach. His non-stop repetitiveness, and use of words, hand gestures, pacing, tone of voice, arrogance, pompousness, candor, rudeness, and disregard for political norms, was all refreshing to me. I was not bored. I started to pay attention. It is almost as if he knew that at some core level the country was bored as f*ck and need to shake things up and get people's attention. And he did that. It still was not enough of a jolt for me to vote for him in 2016. I was not even a fan of Bernie Sanders. I was not entirely on board with his agenda either. Nor was I fan of Hilary Clinton. I think that one Clinton was enough for me in my lifetime, I didn't need to experience another. And it didn't matter that she was a woman. I was not going to vote with my genitals and reproductive organs in mind. Though a female president was appealing to me at one point, when Hilary Clinton ran in 2008 against Barak Obama. But again, I had already decided a long time ago that the election process was rigged. Of course, I let one isolated incident determine my overall outlook on politics and the election process, which I should have gotten over but I didn't. I was still holding on to my beliefs about the Al Gore and Bush debacle.

Therefore, I can somewhat understand how a number of Republican voters feel when they believe that the 2020 election was rigged and continue to push for state election audits. I can understand to a fair extent why some or perhaps many Republican voters are angry and do not accept Biden as their president. Similarly, I understand why, when Trump was elected into office, that there were mass protests across the country, with people holding signs that said, "Not my president." I can understand that completely. I am not sure how many of those people believed that the election was rigged, however. I am curious to know that. But several Democrat voters felt as though the world just ended and that our countries democracy was going down the toilet. I can understand the feelings expressed by people on both sides of the political isle and I am willing to listen to what people have to say with as little judgement as possible. Because I believe this is the time to be more moderate. I believe that the era of the black or white moderate, the male or female or trans, or non-gender specific moderate, is not at all dead. In fact, era is alive and well and ready to create change for the betterment of society. So, perhaps being a New Democrat or moderate is not entirely without its value, meaning, purpose and merit. The New Democrat has its place in politics.

Chapter 6
The Moderate Republicans

During my inquiry into the "black moderate" not only did it learn about the New Democrats, but I also stumbled across this new faction within the Republican Party called the "Moderate Republicans." Naturally, I was curious about this faction and found myself perusing a website dedicated to this faction. For example, according to Moderate-Republicans website, "Moderate Republicans are right-of-center voters in the political spectrum. They are generally considered progressive on the social issues, conservative on the fiscal issues, and typically prioritize fiscal demands over social agenda. Moderate Republicans proudly embrace the tradition of an inclusive party, but seek to reinstate mainstream Republican viewpoints within the elective body and party leadership."[23]

Regarding social issues such as Reproductive Rights, "Moderate Republicans generally support current US law as found in the Supreme Court decisions of Roe v. Wade (1973) and Planned Parenthood of Southeastern Pennsylvania v. Casey (1992). Here the Supreme Court declared that a woman's right to privacy under the Due Process Clause of the 14th Amendment extends to her decision whether or not to terminate a pregnancy. The Supreme Court also said, however, that the woman's right could be balanced against the legitimate state interests of protecting womens' health and the potentiality of human life at the point of fetal viability. Fetal viability was defined as the point at which the fetus is able to live outside the womb with artificial aid. Moderate Republicans believe that banning abortion is a regressive step and outside the proper role of government. They understand that the absence of availability to safe abortion can be a dangerous and destructive force

---

[23] Moderate-Republicans, https://www.moderate-republicans.com/who-we-are

in the lives of many women. Moderate Republicans believe this issue has hindered more important reforms and served to exclude many people from the party, particularly women, for whom the preservation of reproductive rights is a privacy issue of great importance."[24]

Regarding, environment and climate change, "Moderate Republicans recognize scientific evidence demonstrating that human activity is affecting the world's climate. They welcome a healthy debate on this issue, including impacts, strategy, and responsible resource allocation. Moderate Republicans believe that environmental protection is one of our greatest responsibilities. They recognize, however, that as just 5% of the global population, the United States must work with other nations to lead global initiatives and advance its policy through treaties and trade agreements. A global approach will likewise benefit our own companies who deserve a level playing field regarding environmental regulation." [25] What's more, regarding gay rights, "Moderate Republicans generally believe that extending rights enjoyed by all Americans to gay-Americans does not threaten our society. This includes the right to marriage, military service, and adoption. They believe that extending these rights to gay-Americans is the right thing to do and enhances liberty in the United States."[26]

There are many more views that this website shares with the public, such as their views on capital punishment, taxes, education, efficiency in government operations, media, foreign policy and defense spending, privacy, criminal justice reform, trade and currency, social

---

[24] Moderate-Republicans, https://www.moderate-republicans.com/more-views
[25] Moderate-Republicans, https://www.moderate-republicans.com/more-views
[26] Moderate-Republicans, https://www.moderate-republicans.com/more-views

welfare reform, budget process reform, and evolution. Upon reading each of their views and initiatives, I was impressed, to be quite honest. I liked what they had to say. I liked that this organization was pointing out many of the obvious issues which need to be addressed. Towards the end of my time, I read their mission statement, which you may or may not agree with. I, personally, did agree with various aspects of their statement. For instance, according to the Moderate-Republicans their "mission is to organize, educate, and bring identity to right-of-center voters who believe in constitutional principles of limited government and fiscal responsibility, but not the social agenda of the far-right." They "seek to develop deeply informed opinions among" its "members and help bring those opinions to the polls." Their "aim" is "to rebalance the Republican Party to better reflect the demographics of mainstream America, and lead a new era of promoting government efficiency, enhancing democracy, and maximizing personal freedom for all."[27]

I cannot speak for others; however, I can agree that much of what this moderate ideology has to offer is on par with what I consider to be "Classical Republican" ideology. The Republican ideology that dates to Abraham Lincoln. In fact, this new faction seems to model itself haver Lincoln's ideals regarding democracy, equality, freedoms and so forth, which is reflective of "Classical Republicanism." Not this other brand of Republican ideology. And if I were to choose a political faction, I would consider the Moderate-Republican faction. I would also consider the New Democrat faction. Because both seem to hold very similar ideologies and beliefs. Their missions are almost identical. My thought is, if these two factions within their respective parties can manage to get

---

[27] Moderate-Republicans, https://www.moderate-republicans.com/mission

things done on the Hill and within each state, there is a chance for something good to evolve over time that may help bridge the many political gaps this country is presently experiencing, bolstering, fanning the flames of, adding to, or running away from. The fact that people with polarizing political views can't even hold a civil conversation about their views is absolutely abhorrent to me. The fact that two grown adult people, with responsibilities cannot sit face to face and have civil discourse about their views that may lead to a middle ground reflects our collective mental instability in this country, in my humble opinion. Now that comment may not sit well with you. But think about the times you could not have a conversation with this person or that person because they either voted for Trump or voted for Biden.

Furthermore, think about the times you may have been on social media and possibly said some unsavory things about the individual because they either voted for Trump or voted for Biden, depending on which way you lean and what ideologies you subscribe to. It is as if, someone who is extremely Democrat and someone who is extremely Republican believe the other to be living in an alternate reality. I have heard people from both sides of the aisle say that about people who either voted for Trump or voted for Biden. When someone posts something on Facebook for example about their disgust over Fox News, I respond by saying, that there are people on the right that feel the exact same way about CNN. Democrats and Republicans are the yin and yang to each other. One cannot exist without the other. Fox News is the opposite of CNN. Commentators from both news organizations, are opposites of each other. It's all very fascinating to me, now that I can see very clearly the polarization of these two parties and these two news organizations, as an example.

Circling back to the definition of what a Moderate-Republican is, according to them, whoever "they" are, seems as though this faction has more to offer than its farther right Republican counterparts. I suppose the only reservation I have is the fact that "moderate" or not, the faction within the faction that is the Republican Party itself, is still part of the political duopoly. Even Libertarians are part of the duopoly. Though their position is that they are a third political option. However, with all their presidential running, and all their donations, and townhall meetings, and Libertarian candidates, the Libertarian Party does not really stand a chance as a "third party" option the controlled political duopoly. What's more, Libertarians are another faction of the Republican Party in essence, whether some Libertarians want to accept that truth or not. Libertarians lean to the right. Therefore, they are just another layer of the Republican Party and Republicanism as a whole.

If one were to select a "faction" within the faction, be it left or right, one can opt to consider the Moderate-Republican faction or the New Democrat faction as I previously mentioned, because these are the two options might align with your more moderate political beliefs and ideologies. Moreover, these are going to be the two factions, I believe that will do the most work to reach those sitting in the "middle", that are more "centrist" in their views, or perhaps are non-voters on the fence about which party fits well if one fits at all. And it is quite possible that the Moderate-Republicans will do more work to snatch up those individuals. Though, again, moderate, or not, it is still choosing a single party in the end, be it Republican or Democrat. And in the eyes of these more far leaning party members, you will either be considered, or perceived as being a socialist, or a fascist. Either way, you're branded as either one or the other. However, if these two factions work very hard to distance themselves from these polarizing and damaging political beliefs and can stand apart and alone from these two perceptions held tightly by many members of either party, there might be an opportunity to change those perceptions.

To maintain continuity in finding more definitions to the things I am searching, let us review what Wikipedia has to offer about the "Moderate-Republicans." For example, according to Wikipedia, "The Rockefeller Republicans, also called Moderate or Liberal Republicans, were members of the Republican Party (GOP) in the 1930s–1970s who held moderate to liberal views on domestic issues, similar to those of Nelson Rockefeller, Governor of New York (1959–1973) and Vice President of the United States (1974–1977). Rockefeller Republicans were most common in the Northeast, and industrial Midwestern states with their larger liberal constituencies while they were rare in the South and West. The term refers to "[a] member of the Republican Party holding views likened to those of Nelson Rockefeller; a moderate or liberal Republican". However, Geoffrey Kabaservice states that they were part of a separate political ideology, aligning on certain issues and policies with liberals, while on others with conservatives and on many with neither. Luke Phillips has also stated that the Rockefeller Republicans represent the continuation of the Whig tradition of American politics." [28]

Moreover, to briefly summarize what the Whig Party believed, "The Whig Party believed in a strong federal government, similar to the Federalist Party that preceded it. The federal government must provide

---

[28] "Rockefeller Republican": *Wikipedia*,
https://en.wikipedia.org/wiki/Rockefeller_Republican#:~:text=The%20Rockef eller%20Republicans%2C%20also%20called,States%20(1974%E2%80%931977).

its citizenry with a transportation infrastructure to assist economic development. Many Whigs also called for government support of business through tariffs." [29] Sound familiar? The more classical Republican ideology comes from the Whigs and the Federalists. You can see how things shape shifted over the past one hundred to two hundred years in this country regarding its political identities. These identities continued to shift around so much so that there was virtually, what some would argue, a complete change in "political platform" or "party platform." Additionally, regarding the Whig Party, "at the same time that the Whig Party formed, the Democratic Party also existed. The Democrats, as a whole, believed that the states should retain as much power as possible. The federal government should only have a bare minimum number of powers, and these powers should consist only of ones necessary for the federal government to function. The Democrats emphasized the rights of the common people, a message that was especially receptive among small farmers and factory workers. The Democratic Party also called for the United States' expansion. This would open up new land for settlement, a message that struggling farmers and factory workers, who hoped to own their own land someday, welcomed."[30]

If you read the language closely in the previous passage, you can surmise that those who argue that the two political party platforms changed, are not entirely wrong. However, let's read it again, only I am going to change some things around, so that we can see the parallelism. For example, currently, the (Republicans, as a whole, believe that the states should retain as much power as possible. The federal government

---

[29] *Whig Party*, https://ohiohistorycentral.org/w/Whig_Party
[30] *Whig Party*, https://ohiohistorycentral.org/w/Whig_Party

should only have a bare minimum number of powers, and these powers should consist only of ones necessary for the federal government to function. The Republicans emphasize the rights of the common people, a message that was especially receptive among small farmers and factory workers.) Similarly, Trump championed limiting federal powers, bolstering state rights, and catering to the small farmers and factory workers, bringing jobs back to America, and to "Make America Great Again."

Chapter 7

The Centrists

For many years I was a registered Democrat. In 2008, I registered as an Independent. Then in 2018, I became a registered in Pennsylvania as an Independent. During the summer of 2018, I changed my party affiliation to Republican. Later that same year, I changed my affiliation again back to Democrat. Then changed it again, back to Republican. Then changed it again to Libertarian. Then changed it gain to "Independent." All these changes occurred in 2018. I know. It is confusing. Why did I bounce back and forth like this? I was going through a political identity-crisis myself. I was reading and writing, engaging with others and blogging about various political topics. One minute my views aligned with the Democrat views. The next it aligned with Republican views. Then I read about Libertarians and decided that registering as a Libertarian is a better fit. But eventually, it no longer fit. Then I finally settled on "Non-affiliation"/ "Independent" voter registration. The truth is, being an "Independent" or "Non-affiliation" voter, there is no representation. It's kind of like being politically homeless in a way. There is no National Committee for Independents. There is no Super PAC, or PAC, or any figure head or group to organize the "Independents" of this country or mobilize us in any way. We are left wandering the political streets in search of a place to call home. But no home presents itself.

This feeling of political homelessness may make one feel left out of the political fold entirely. Especially, during the primaries because we can't vote in the primaries as independents. Of course, being the politically unaware person that I was for so long, and without this knowledge, I did try and vote in the primary election in 2016. When I walked inside the building of which ballots were being cast, the woman told me that I could not vote. I stood there and asked her why? She informed me that this is the "primary" election and that I have to either be a registered Democrat or registered Republican to vote in the primary election. Now you may be thinking, that should have already known that. But I didn't. When I walked out of the building, I stood there feeling baffled and confused. Then another person walked out shaking his head. And he proceeded to blurt out, "this is bullshit." I responded, "I know", without knowing what his comment was in reference to, but I had a gut feeling it was because he too was an independent voter and could vote in the primary. I asked him if he was an independent and was turned away. He exclaimed that he was and that it's bullshit that "independent voters" cannot vote in the primary.

Fast forward, I understand why independents cannot vote in the primary. But at the time, I thought being unable to vote in the primary as a "non-affiliation" voter was bullshit too. But I get it. The point is, as a political Centrist, that I identify myself as being, I should be able to vote in the primary. Because there were other candidates to choose from. In other words, whomever Republican voters select during the primaries and whomever Democrat voters select during the primaries, we "non-affiliates" are stuck with the choices presented, unless we vote for the Libertarian candidate or the Green Party candidate, which we can certainly do. There are no rules to who we wish to vote for. People on the right and left may criticize the "non-affiliate" voting for the Green Party candidate or the Libertarian candidate because they hold to the belief that, since we voted for the "other" person, that is a vote that could have gone to "this Democrat candidate" or "that Republican candidate." In sum, we are potentially viewed as the people who "cost them an election." Which I think is a bit extreme. But this is how we are viewed if we voted for the "other" candidate. And I did vote for the "other" candidate.

Admittedly, I voted for Gary Johnson in the 2016 election. I wasn't thrilled about either Trump or Clinton to be quite honest. And there are those individuals that give me the side eye or try to lecture me about how I am supposed to vote or feel as though they are obligated to spread their political beliefs to others for the betterment of society, which I find to be arrogant, narcissistic, and wildly inappropriate. I don't ask people who they voted for. It is none of my business. However, several people felt they were justified in asking who I voted for. And I agreed to share, only to be met with ridicule and disapproval. Moreover, I felt violated in a small way, feeling as if I owe people an explanation. I wish I had the gumption and the guts enough to tell those handful of folks to f*ck off. But I didn't. Now, at this point in my life, I would graciously, and with love, to f*ck off. I have no problem telling individuals who want to know who I am voting for or who I voted for, that it's not anyone's business who I voted for. I have had to politely say that to others while I am in their home, or at a dinner, or at work.

The point of this blathering about my experience and explaining my feeling of political homelessness and the concept of centrism, is that there ought to be clarity with what Centrism means. Therefore, for the sake of continued continuity, Wikipedia defines Centrism as "a political outlook or position that involves acceptance and/or support of a balance of social equality and a degree of social hierarchy, while opposing political changes which would result in a significant shift of society strongly to either the left or the right. Both centre-left and centre-right politics involve a general association with centrism that is combined with leaning somewhat to their respective sides of the left–right political spectrum. Various political ideologies, such as Christian democracy and social (or modern) liberalism, can be classified as centrist ones, as can the Third Way, a modern political movement that attempts to reconcile right-wing and left-wing politics by advocating for a synthesis of centre-right economic platforms with some centre-left social policies."[31]

Furthermore, according to Encyclopedia, "politics, centrism refers to the tendency to avoid political extremes by taking an ideologically intermediate position. A centrist promotes moderate policies by finding a middle ground between the left and the right and downplays ideological appeals in favor of a pragmatic or "catchall" party platform. Centrism can be seen as a means to maximize electoral support, especially among swing voters (those who will vote across party lines). The left-right political spectrum is a traditional way of classifying ideologies, political positions, or political parties. The terms left, right, and center are believed to originate from the manner in which parliamentary factions were seated in the French Convention after the Revolution of 1789. Seated on the left were radicals such as the Montagnards and the Jacobins, who wanted to abolish the monarchy, the aristocracy, and even religion in France. Seated on the right were royalists and conservatives such as the Feuillants, who supported the king and the Catholic Church. Seated in the center were moderate republicans like the Girondins, who wanted to abolish the Bourbon monarchy but opposed radical demands for revolutionary terror and exporting the revolution to the rest of Europe."[32]

---

[31] "Centrism", *Wikipedia*, https://en.wikipedia.org/wiki/Centrism
[32] "Centrism", *Encyclopedia*, https://www.encyclopedia.com/social-sciences/applied-and-social-sciences-magazines/centrism

What's more, "in contrast to the center, both the left and the right are understood to represent well-defined political positions, or ideologies, that are polar opposites of each other. The left-right spectrum is linked to the rise of three main ideologies—conservatism, liberalism, and socialism. Conservatism is associated today with a right-wing stance; conservative ideology resists progressive social change and tries to conserve the status quo, or bring back the status quo ante of the ancien regime. Those to the right of conservatives are sometimes called ultraconservatives or the Far Right; These labels may refer to fascists, national socialists (Nazis), ultranationalists, religious extremists, and other reactionaries. Next to emerge was liberalism, which situates itself in the center of the political arena, claiming to be moderate, reformist, and thus centrist. The last of the three ideologies to arise, socialism is commonly seen as left-wing or radical, because socialists view themselves as the radical or militant heirs of the French Revolution. Unlike self-styled centrist liberals, socialists believe that social progress cannot always be achieved by gradualist liberal reforms alone and may require radical social change or even social revolution. Those to the left of socialists are typically labeled ultra-leftists or the Far Left, often referring to anarchists, Communists, Trotskyists, Maoists, and other extreme leftists."[33]

Moreover, "Center-leaning politicians or parties usually seek compromise between conflicting political extremes and often take middle-of-the-road stances designed to bridge opposite ideological camps. Political centrism is thus by definition a relational concept,

---

[33] "Centrism", *Encyclopedia*, https://www.encyclopedia.com/social-sciences/applied-and-social-sciences-magazines/centrism

because the positions considered centrist depend on the specific policies of the competing ideological poles that the moderates are trying to reconcile. Centrism is important in the early twenty-first century because it is believed to apply to a very large section of the politically active population. In many countries, most members of the voting public tend to identify themselves as independent rather than as either left-wing or right-wing. The Economist stated in April 2005, "Most Americans have fairly centrist views on everything from multiculturalism to abortion. They like to think of themselves as 'moderate' and 'non-judgmental.' More people identify themselves as independents (39%, according to the Pew Research Centre for the People & the Press) than as Democrats (31%) or Republicans (30%)." Politicians of various parties thus try to appeal to this presumed majority in the center to reach beyond their traditional, narrow constituencies and win elections. Left-wing and right-wing parties dilute their more extreme positions, for both know that the bulk of voters are somewhere near the center. With ideological considerations toned down, centrism tends to make politics more tranquil and stable. The post–cold war decline of left-right divisions has hastened the spread of a new centrist ideology, which is more supportive of democracy and capitalism."[34]

In sum, "this center-seeking or centripetal approach entails some risk. Candidates advocating centrist policies to gain wider voter appeal risk demobilizing potential voters and losing support from the more ideologically minded partisans of their own party. Calling itself "New Labour," the revamped British Labour Party won three successive general elections, but voter turnout declined from 71.29 percent in 1997

---

[34] "Centrism", *Encyclopedia*, https://www.encyclopedia.com/social-sciences/applied-and-social-sciences-magazines/centrism

to 61.36 percent in 2005, as Prime Minister Tony Blair's policy of abandoning key socialist tenets and embracing the center ground alienated many Labour loyalists." [35] And given that the "revamped British Labour Party" rebranded itself as the "New Labour" party abandoning some of its "key socialist tenets", it makes sense that the faction the "New Democrats" has taken shape and become a third way just left of center on the political spectrum. Similarly, it makes sense that the faction the "Moderate Republicans" has taken shape and become a fifth way just right of center on the political spectrum.

Circling back to the statement from the dream, "the era of the black moderate is dead" is not entirely so. That was a position she took. But that is not a position I need to take. Because it is obvious to me that the era of the "moderate" is not dead and is in a state of renewal and rebirth. But as I write these words, I am remembering that this person is a person who sits to the far left of the political spectrum. Her statement aligns with her political beliefs. Therefore, her I understand why she made the statement in the first place. However, death is just another door to a new chapter. And the era of the New Democrat and the Moderate Republican is right now. The only caveat with these two right of center and left of center factions is that the people the select to represent them as presidential candidates are not center left or center right. They are either on the farther left or farther right. There is not a middle in these selections, therefore, selecting a presidential candidate who is either a true to form Democrat or true to form Republican, if you are a centrist, is extremely difficult because you may not agree with either candidate;

---

[35] "Centrism", *Encyclopedia*, https://www.encyclopedia.com/social-sciences/applied-and-social-sciences-magazines/centrism

your stuck with who is on the ballot sheet. And I for one, am tired of being "stuck" with whomever these parties choose during the primaries. Hence my discontent over this political duopoly that for some reason, our country cannot break free from. It's a form of political enslavement. And that is why I have come to the belief that political beliefs in general, are nothing more than psychosocial constructs. What you put into either system of belief becomes your reality. And I am stuck with other people's reality, politically speaking. That must change. It's time for a third way; a third "real" candidate.

Part Two–

The Psychosocial Construct

"Let us not seek the Republican answer or the Democratic answer, but the right answer. Let us not seek to fix the blame for the past. Let us accept our own responsibility for the future."

— John F. Kennedy

Chapter 8

The Horseshoe Theory

Here we are. And you may be wondering what the "horseshoe theory" is. For a moment, let us go back to the subtitle of this book, "the psychosocial construct of political beliefs." The term psychosocial in psychology is "describing the intersection and interaction of social, cultural, and environmental influences on the mind and behavior."[36] The term construct is "an idea or theory containing various conceptual elements, typically one considered to be subjective and not based on empirical evidence." [37] Regarding politics, one could argue that democracy is an ideological construct. And I would have to agree. However, when we think about political beliefs, one might not consider a political belief to be a "construct" or an idea that is based in the hypothetical, something that is not tangible. Yet, a political belief, in my potentially subjective opinion, is just that. A construct. Why? Because beliefs are the psychosocial constructs for which I speak a term in psychology that describes the intersection and interaction of social, cultural, and environmental which influence the mind and behavior, which influence, mental attitudes, thought processes, expectations of others and of oneself, pre-judgements, community standards, educational standards, laws, rules, legislative policies, health, medicine, medical procedures, so on and so forth.

Connecting the dots, we can see that a "political idea" or "political belief" both of which are "intangibles", are in fact, "constructs", ideas erected in one's mind. From the collective standpoint, if several people hold the same belief, the same political construct, such

---

[36] "Psychosocial", *APA Dictionary of Psychology*,
https://dictionary.apa.org/psychosocial
[37] "Construct", *Oxford Languages, Google*

as Republicanism, then all those individuals share a common psychosocial construct. Similarly, if several people hold the same belief, the same political construct, such as Democratism, then all those individuals share a common psychosocial construct. Moreover, if several people hold the same belief, the same political construct, such as Centrism, then all those individuals share a common psychosocial construct. So, you, see? Most everyone is a part of the many political psychosocial constructs, in almost every country that has some form of a government. The point here is that we do not have to over invest ourselves into these constructs, knowing what they are from a psychological level to the point where people find their identity in various political factions, in various political leaders, figure heads and actors/actresses.

What's more, one can cancel their psychosocial subscription any time they want. No one is being forced to be a Republican, a Democrat, a New Democrat, a Moderate Republican, or a Centrist, or a "non-voter." We are all choosing these political beliefs, ideologies, and constructs for ourselves. However, it is possible that some people have blindly chosen a political construct because everyone around them is either a Democrat or a Republican so by default they are one or the either depending. And if you notice, all of these constructs are purely based in the external world but are completely subject to one's imagination. Because the truth is, political beliefs are not anything at all. They are someone else's theories, ideals, beliefs, and ideologies, handed down from one generation to the next. They are taught in schools, so we are all indoctrinated into a political belief from early childhood. They are marketed in television advertisements, news headlines and articles, plastered onto billboards lining miles of a highway, they are preached in the pulpits of every church in America, they are propagated by every elected official. They are our countries, motto, and military tenets. They are enshrined in the halls of every Federal Building. There is no escaping these constructs because they are everywhere we look. In essence, we have all been brainwashed into believing these constructs are real. So much so that even these constructs have smaller constructs within the main construct. In other words, the factions which exist within the factions themselves, have become so concentrated in their identities, beliefs, ideologies, tenets, goals, that they have become problematic.

For example, think about the political spectrum in the shape of a horseshoe. At the top of the horseshoe is "Centrism" on the bottom left is "communism" and at the bottom right, "fascism." Then there is all the stuff between these three points. What is fascinating, is that the two bottom ends of the horseshoe are very close to each other. Almost mirroring one another in some way. It's more than political polarities. The horseshoe theory is about exposing similarities of the extremes. For instance, "The horseshoe theory, also known as the horseshoe effect, in political science is a claim that the far-left and far-right are more similar to each other in essentials than either is to the political center. It was formulated by the French post-postmodernist philosopher Jean-Pierre Faye in 1996, but similar ideas existed previously. Faye believed that the extremes of the political spectrum both represented totalitarianism of different kinds; this meant that the political spectrum should not be described as a linear bar with the two ends representing the far-left and right being ideologically the furthest apart from each other, but as a horseshoe in which the two ends are closer to each other than to the center."[38]

However, the horseshoe theory has garnered much criticism in American politics. Many oppose the idea that the two political extremes are one and the same essentially. Yet, one can argue that the political extremes one being communism and the other fascism are in fact two sides of the same coin. For example, according to the 2018 "left leaning publication" Pacific Standard article, "Let's put an end to the Horseshoe Theory once and for all", Noah Berlatsky asserts that "the main argument for Horseshoe Theory is that both the far left and the far right are opposed to the centrist, neoliberal/capitalist status quo. Communists and fascists in the 1930s criticized the aging imperial democracies of Britain, France, and the United States as weak, corrupt, and—post-Great Depression— as hurtling toward a final collapse. More recently, the argument goes, left-wing radicals opposed centrist Hillary Clinton and France's Emmanuel Macron. By doing so, they offered de facto (and sometimes more than de facto) aid to racist, nationalist opponents like Trump and Marine Le Pen. We are told that left and right both want to destroy democratic norms and the sensible center. Therefore, Horseshoe Theory says, they work together."[39]

The criticisms of the Horseshoe Theory seem sound. For instance, according to history professor Christopher Muscato of University of Northern Colorado, asserts that "the first argument against horseshoe theory is that, while the extreme left and right may both

---

[38] "Horseshoe Theory", *RationalWiki*,
https://rationalwiki.org/wiki/Horseshoe_theory
[39] Berlatsky, Noah, "Let's put an end to the horseshoe theory once and for all", *Pacific Standard*, https://psmag.com/social-justice/an-end-to-horseshoe-theory

become authoritarian, their actual reasons for doing so are incompatible. They both justify and wield centralized political power in very different ways. The best way to see this is through example. Fascists and communists both stress a strongly centralized government and a collective over individualistic sense of self, right? However:

- Fascists do so for the sake of nationalism, security, and generally ethnic pride.

- Communists centralize the state around the concept of wealth distribution and suppress individualism as a way to support a collective, classless economy.

In practice, these systems have completely different goals, even if some of their means are similar. In issues facing the modern world, we can see the incompatibility of the extreme left and right in dealing with globalism. Globalism, as supported by the center, is something that both extremes tend to reject. Again, however, their reasoning and solutions are very different.

- The extreme right sees globalism as a threat to national security, national identity, and national purity. Their goal is to stop globalism, build stronger borders, and generally become more isolationist.

- The extreme left sees globalism as an entrenchment of class systems and oppression of developing states under industrialized, capitalist ones. Their solution is not to eliminate globalism, but to reform it and remove the influences of capitalism."[40]

---

[40] Muscato, Christopher, "Criticism of the Horseshoe Theory", *Study.com*, https://study.com/academy/lesson/criticism-of-the-horseshoe-theory.html

Professor Muscato continues in his assessment by stating that "the second, albeit slightly less popular, criticism of the horseshoe theory is that its only true function is to serve the center. In this criticism, opponents of horseshoe theory see this model as a way to oversimplify extreme viewpoints, and thereby make them look simply evil and the center inherently good. Basically, by claiming that all extreme views are basically the same, the theory lets people in the center dismiss these views as oppressive and violent without really having to understand them. Were the Soviets and Nazis violent and oppressive? Yes, they were, but critics of horseshoe theory say these qualities are not unique to the far left and far right. The centrist-left and centrist-right are just as capable of being brutal, violent, and oppressive. Even the USA demonstrated great violence against peaceful civil rights protestors in the 1960s. These critics believe that the horseshoe theory is simply a way to marginalize views that the center considers to be extreme. To them, there's nothing lucky about this horseshoe."[41]

Regarding the second argument in which Muscato makes, there are aspects that I do agree with. For example, being the "Centrist" leaning Left and Right, depending on the issues, I agree that all extreme views are equally damaging, harmful and does not serve the greater good of both humanity and of this country. I further agree that these extreme views be them community or fascist are both oppressive and violent, or resort to oppressive and violent tactics to each their goals. Regardless of the nuances in which Muscato pointed about regarding the first argument pertaining to the goals of the "Horseshoe Theory", the polar opposing

---

[41] Muscato, Christopher, "Criticism of the Horseshoe Theory", *Study.com*, https://study.com/academy/lesson/criticism-of-the-horseshoe-theory.html

extremist views of communism and fascism are equally abhorrent positions. But we do in fact, have that ten percent of people which represent these extreme views. As my counterpart always says, "there's a bottom ten percent, a top ten percent and everyone else in between." And he is correct. Because in the world of percentages, in which I live, there is that smaller percentage of people in the extreme left and extreme right. Then, there is everyone else between these two extremes which do not subscribe to such extreme views. That is why we have facts such as the New Democrats and the Moderate Republicans. Essentially, these two factions represent "moderation" in their views entirely. Which I find to be a good thing. This helps bridge many legislative gaps in both the House and the Senate. At this point we very much need more bipartisanism and champions of bipartisanship. That is how our government can effectively govern, in my subjective opinion.

Though there are critics who disagree with the "Horseshoe Theory", there are aspects of this theory which apply. The nuance arguments that others propose are, in my mind, not enough to completely dismantle this theory or render it inapplicable, or illogical, or illegitimate, or inaccurate, or invalid. Though a theory by definition is "a supposition or a system of ideas intended to explain something, especially one based on general principles independent of the thing to be explained,"[42] then, the "Horseshoe Theory" does, on a number of levels, explain the polarities and similarities between the extreme left, (communism) and the extreme right, (fascism), factions. The polarities and similarities are undeniable. Those, in my humble opinion, who argue that these two extremes are not at all similar are in denial themselves.

---

[42] "Theory", *Oxford Languages, Google*

The nuances regarding the "why" may be enough of a differential margin for one to argue that these two extremes are not at all the same. But we are not discussing the nuances. We are discussing the entirety of these two extremes. We are looking at the bigger picture. Therefore, when one person on the left says, "the extreme right are evil fascists, Nazi's who want to turn America into an authoritarian dictatorship", someone on the right equally says, "the extreme left are evil communist Nazi's who want to turn America into an authoritarian dictatorship." To argue over the nuances of these beliefs is counterproductive in this case. We are better off accepting the fact that two extremes are largely one in the same.

Chapter 9
The Construct of Communism

In political discussion there is much debate about if this country is becoming a communist country. Several Republicans believe that this country is in fact turning into a communist country, one in which we allow undocumented immigrants to come into the country and taxpayers have to take care of. While the government has been mailing out stimulus checks and child tax credit checks, some argue that is inflating the National Debt and that the rich will be the ones to have to foot the bill with increased taxes. More Republicans argue that the Biden Administration is running this country into the ground. Conversely, several people on the left believed, while Trump was in office, that this country was turning into a fascist country, on in which we allow white supremacists to feel emboldened to treat black and brown people terribly, one in which unjustified killing of black and brown people by police will remain unchecked, one in which hate crimes remain thematic in our society. And while the government during the Trump Administration had been cutting taxes, adding sanctions and tariffs, and allowing for more oil drilling, Democrats argued that the Trump Administration was running this country into the ground.

However, with regards to "communism", I do believe that is a bit of a stretch given the very nature of what this construct implies. For example, "Communism is a political and economic ideology that positions itself in opposition to liberal democracy and capitalism, advocating instead for a classless system in which the means of production are owned communally and private property is nonexistent or severely curtailed."[43]

---

[43] Chen, James, "Communism", *Investopedia*,
https://www.investopedia.com/terms/c/communism.asp

"KEY TAKEAWAYS

- Communism is an economic ideology that advocates for a classless society in which all property and wealth are communally-owned, instead of by individuals.

- The communist ideology was developed by Karl Marx and Friedrich Engels and is the opposite of a capitalist one, which relies on democracy and production of capital to form a society.

- Prominent examples of communism were the Soviet Union and China. While the former collapsed in 1991, the latter has drastically revised its economic system to include elements of capitalism."[44]

What's more, ""Communism" is an umbrella term that encompasses a range of ideologies. The term's modern usage originated with Victor d'Hupay, an 18th-century French aristocrat who advocated living in "communes" in which all property would be shared, and "all may benefit from everybody's work." The idea was hardly new even at that time, however: the Book of Acts describes first-century Christian communities holding property in common according to a system known as koinonia, which inspired later religious groups such as the 17th-century English "Diggers" to reject private ownership."[45]

Moreover, to gain a bit more insight into the construct of communism, we must defer to the "Communist Manifesto". For instance, "modern communist ideology began to develop during the

---

[44] Chen, James, "Communism", *Investopedia*,
https://www.investopedia.com/terms/c/communism.asp
[45] Chen, James, "Communism", *Investopedia*,
https://www.investopedia.com/terms/c/communism.asp

French Revolution, and its seminal tract, Karl Marx and Friedrich Engels' "Communist Manifesto," was published in 1848. That pamphlet rejected the Christian tenor of previous communist philosophies, laying out a materialist and—its proponents claim—scientific analysis of the history and future trajectory of human society. "The history of all hitherto existing society," Marx and Engels wrote, "is the history of class struggles." The Communist Manifesto presented the French Revolution as a major historical turning point, when the "bourgeoisie" —the merchant class that was in the process of consolidating control over the "means of production" —overturned the feudal power structure and ushered in the modern, capitalist era. That revolution replaced the medieval class struggle, which pitted the nobility against the serfs, with the modern one pitting the bourgeois owners of capital against the "proletariat," the working class who sell their labor for wages.

In the Communist Manifesto and later works, Marx, Engels, and their followers advocated (and predicted as historically inevitable) a global proletarian revolution, which would usher in first an era of socialism, then of communism. This final stage of human development would mark the end of class struggle and therefore of history: all people would live in social equilibrium, without class distinctions, family structures, religion, or property. The state, too, would "wither away." The economy would function, as a popular Marxist slogan puts it, "from each according to his ability, to each according to his needs.""[46]

However, you and I can certainly agree that a communist country is not a solution to any governmental problem. And I do not

---

[46] Chen, James, "Communism", *Investopedia*,
https://www.investopedia.com/terms/c/communism.asp

believe that is where we are headed given our rights and freedoms in this country, rights and freedoms which some Republicans believe are being stripped away. Though "hate speech" has been a prominent force on social media most exclusively during the Trump Administration, stripping away the right of Free speech is not actually happening. Adding laws pertaining to assault rifles and automatic weapons that curtail the purchase of these items in this country is not stripping away of someone's right to bear arms. And one has to keep in mind that when these Constitutional Rights were being drafted, Facebook, Twitter, Youtube and other social media platforms did not exist, all of which are privately owned and have nothing to do with the first amendment. What's more, automatic weapons, semi-automatic weapons, AR-15's, assault rifles of sorts, did not exist. When the Constitution was being drafted people of that time were using muskets, long rifles, bayonets, all of which had to be manually loaded. Illegal gun purchases in the United States remains a constant which contribute to the rise in gun violence in urban communities and cities, as does mass shootings with the use of AR-15's and AK 47's.

Therefore, when critically think about the idea that this country is turning into a communist country, you may arrive to a similar conclusion, that is not an accurate statement to make given the fact that we still have our right to free speech and the right to bear arms, civil and equal rights. The last I checked; those things were still in place. I do not think, believe, or feel, that this country will ever become a communist country. Yet, several people who lean to the right on the political spectrum, deeply feel and believe that this country, while under the rule and reign of the Democrat Party, will one day, become a Communist Country, and it is their patriotic duty to vote for Trump and or anyone who upholds "Americanism" not "Communism." But some believe that one day this country will become like China. There has been talk amongst various conspiracy theorists that Biden has strong ties to China and because of his alleged relationship with leaders of China or whoever, that those alleged allegiances and associations will pave the path towards communism. I am not entirely sure where some people have gotten their information. Much of it I'm sure is highly questionable. Yet, some folks believe in this narrative. And for a moment or two, I believe the conspiratorial rhetoric myself. It is quite contagious when you're around conspiracy theorists, especially if you're a person who has an addiction problem.

As began to wean myself off the conspiratorial crack pipe, I began to think rationally, logically, and critically again. I no lingered harbored the opinion or belief that this country was going to become like China. But I do think that anything is possible. And to pull off a magic trick like that, would require planning and timing. The process would have to happen gradually and strategically. But again, I do not think that is our trajectory. However, to I think it is worthwhile to review some of the aspects of Communist China. For instance, "in 1949, following more than 20 years of war with the Chinese Nationalist Party and Imperial Japan, Mao Zedong's Communist Party gained control of China to form the world's second major Marxist-Leninist state. Mao allied the country with the Soviet Union, but the Soviets' policies of de-Stalinization and "peaceful coexistence" with the capitalist West led to a diplomatic split with China in 1956.

Mao's rule in China resembled Stalin's in its violence, deprivation, and insistence on ideological purity. During the Great Leap Forward from 1958 to 1962, the Communist Party ordered the rural population to produce enormous quantities of steel in an effort to jumpstart an industrial revolution in China. Families were coerced into building backyard furnaces, where they smelted scrap metal and household items into low-quality pig iron that offered little domestic utility and held no appeal for export markets. Since rural labor was unavailable to harvest crops, and Mao insisted on exporting grain to demonstrate his policies' success, food became scarce. The resulting Great Chinese Famine killed at least 15 million people and perhaps more than 45 million. The Cultural Revolution, an ideological purge that lasted from 1966 until Mao's death in 1976, killed at least another 400,000 people.

After Mao's death, Deng Xiaoping introduced a series of market reforms that have remained in effect under his successors. The U.S. began normalizing relations with China when President Nixon visited in 1972, prior to Mao's death. The Chinese Communist Party remains in power, presiding over a largely capitalist system, though state-owned enterprises continue to form a large part of the economy. Freedom of expression is significantly curtailed; elections are banned (except in the former British colony of Hong Kong, where candidates must be approved by the party and voting rights are tightly controlled); and meaningful opposition to the party is not permitted."[47]

What I find interesting in about this communist country are political aspects such as "candidates must be approved by the party and voting rights are tightly controlled." That sounds eerily like what this country is presently experiencing with regards to voter rights changes in

---

[47] Chen, James, "Communism", *Investopedia*,
https://www.investopedia.com/terms/c/communism.asp

various states, being tightly controlled by the state. But our elections are not banned, and we all do have the freedom of expression. Even if our expressions are in opposition of each other. Ultimately, communism would fail in the United States. There are too many aspects about communism that will not ever work. Furthermore, referring to the example of The Cold War, The Cold War eventually ended and collapsed the Soviet Union in 1991. Some of the reasons communism may fail or has failed, is because "first is an absence of incentives among citizens to produce for profit. The profit incentive leads to competition and innovation in society. But an ideal citizen in a communist society was selflessly devoted to societal causes and rarely stopped to think about his or her welfare. "At all times and all questions, a party member should give first consideration to the interests of the Party as a whole and put them in the foremost and place personal matters and interests second," wrote Liu Shaoqi, the second chair of the People's Republic of China.

The second reason for communism's failure was the system's inherent inefficiencies, such as centralized planning. This form of planning requires aggregation and synthesis of enormous amounts of data at a granular level. Because all projects were planned centrally, this form of planning was also complex. In several instances, growth data was fudged or error-prone in order to make facts fit into planned statistics and create an illusion of progress."[48] Lastly, "the concentration of power into the hands of select few also bred inefficiency and, paradoxically enough, provided them with incentives to game the system for their benefit and retain their hold on power. Corruption and laziness

---

[48] Chen, James, "Communism", *Investopedia*,
https://www.investopedia.com/terms/c/communism.asp

became endemic features of this system and surveillance, such as the one that characterized East German and Soviet societies, was common. It also disincentivized industrious and hard-working people. The end result was that the economy suffered."[49]

[49] Chen, James, "Communism", *Investopedia*,
https://www.investopedia.com/terms/c/communism.asp

Chapter 10

The Construct of Fascism

Can the construct of Communism exist without the construct of fascism? Would not the two constructs fit together like and hand in glove? For example, "Fascism is a form of far-right, authoritarian ultranationalism characterized by dictatorial power, forcible suppression of opposition, and strong regimentation of society and of the economy, which came to prominence in early 20th-century Europe." [50] And "Communism is a political and economic ideology that positions itself in opposition to liberal democracy and capitalism, advocating instead for a classless system in which the means of production are owned communally, and private property is nonexistent or severely curtailed."[51] Taking a closer look at these two seemingly polarizing constructs, they both equate to totalitarianism expressed in two destructive and dehumanizing ways. For instance, according to the 2017 The Daily Beast article, "Communism and Fascism: The Reason They Are So Similar", J.P. O'Malley asserts that "two 20th-century ideologies promised a utopian vision that would ensure infinite happiness. They both stemmed from a political, social, and cultural construct that erased traditional ideas regarding good and evil. Both believed in the destruction of the old world, to build a new international order; each deplored what they saw as the pathetic ennui of bourgeoisie existence; each ideology's shared purpose was to recruit members of the new utopia. Those ideologies happen to be communism and fascism, which together brought an orgy of violence, killed millions, and led humanity to its darkest hour, where the final destination was the deplorable Gulags and the gas chambers of Auschwitz."[52]

Fascism at its core is defined by National Socialism by race and Communism is at its core is defined by class. However, both ideological constructs, at their core, are defined by power and control of the one or few, which is the definition of authoritarianism or a dictatorship. Therefore, in many keyways these two political and psychosocial constructs share insidious similarities. Because a dictatorship does not

---

[50] "Fascism", *Wikipedia*
[51] Chen, James, "Communism", *Investopedia*,
https://www.investopedia.com/terms/c/communism.asp
[52] O'Malley, J.P., "Communism and Fascism: The Reason They Are So Similar",
The Daily Beast, https://www.thedailybeast.com/communism-and-fascism-the-reason-they-are-so-similar

have to come in the form of one individual. A dictatorship can also come in the form of a collective body, or an elite ruling class. However, senior writer, Wendy Weisberger at Live Science, in her article, "What is fascism?", asserts that "Fascism is a political ideology that's actually pretty difficult to define."[53] Weisberger, asks, "how is fascism defined? Robert Paxton, a professor emeritus of social science at Columbia University in New York, who is widely considered the father of fascism studies, told Live Science that fascism is "a form of political practice distinctive to the 20th century that arouses popular enthusiasm by sophisticated propaganda techniques."

According to Paxton, fascism uses such propaganda to promote:

- anti-liberalism, rejecting individual rights, civil liberties, free enterprise and democracy

- anti-socialism, rejecting economic principles based on socialist frameworks

- exclusion of certain groups, often through violence

- nationalism that seeks to expand the nation's influence and power"[54]

What's more, according to Wikipedia, "Fascism is a form of far-right, authoritarian ultranationalism characterized by dictatorial power, forcible suppression of opposition, and strong regimentation of society and of the economy, which came to prominence in early 20th-century Europe."[55] So when some Democrat voters say that Trump is a fascist and a dictator, given how, on the surface, Trump has handled many different difficult situations such as social injustice, anti-Semitism,

[53] Weisberger, Wendy, "What is Fascism?", *Live Science*, https://www.livescience.com/57622-fascism.html
[54] Weisberger, Wendy, "What is Fascism?", *Live Science*, https://www.livescience.com/57622-fascism.html
[55] "Fascism", *Wikipedia*

racism, and undocumented immigrants, one could agree that Trump's behavior resembles the behaviors of Mussolini, Mao, or Hitler. Conversely, some Republican voters do not see Trump's behavior resembling the behaviors of any of these men. They regard Trump's behavior pertaining to "Making America Great Again", as the behavior of a true leader, a patriot, and someone who truly loves this country. Members of the voter public that subscribe to the construct of Republicanism, regard Trump as a hero, and a person who stands up to anything. In the farther right evangelical circles, Trump is regarded as God's chosen one. The amount of blind dedication, by "supporters", to a man who has dedicated his entire life to the advancement of himself, without regard to others, characteristic of narcissistic behavior, is most uncanny.

Now, of the seventy million people that voted for Trump this recent election, may have only voted for him because they believe he is the better candidate when it comes to the "business" of The United States. For example, I have one friend who voted for Trump in 2016, that believed he was the better candidate for the job because he is a businessman, not a politician. My friend said that he voted with his pockets. This individual is not a "Trumpian." He is a fiscally conservative, socially moderate Republican voter and has been for some time. He does not subscribe to the ideology of "Trumpism." And there are several Republicans who voted in the same manner as my friend who do not subscribe to the construct of "Trumpism." However, Democrat voters, may not view those Republican voters in a fiscally conservative, socially moderate light. Instead, those Democrat voters will believe those Republican voters to be "fascists" themselves, for voting for a "fascist." Interestingly, when we look at what the construct of fascism is, as previously outlined, there are a couple of key bullet points which conflict with the theory that Trump is a fascist.

For example, "according to Paxton, fascism uses such propaganda to promote:

- anti-liberalism, rejecting individual rights, civil liberties, free enterprise and democracy."[56]

The points about rejection of individual rights, civil liberties, and free enterprise, do not fit within the framework that is "Trumpism" that some believe is synonymous with "fascism." If Trump were truly a fascist as some claim, he himself would not be promoting free enterprise, and individual rights. Because these two aspects of his campaign and presumably his presidency were predicated upon the political precepts of individual rights and free enterprise. In sum, a true fascist does in fact reject individual rights and free enterprise. We can both agree that Trump being a businessman, presumably not a very good one by some standards, is about making money. Arguably, Trump has always been about making money and having more power. And what do all men with power want? More power. Therefore, it is no wonder that Trump has had his eye on a presidency since the 1980s. It is no surprise that he finally decided to run for office. And it is no surprise that he changed his voter registration from Democrat to Republican and ran as a Republican candidate on the ballot sheet. Trump is a smart man in several ways pertaining to marketing and again, making money.

---

[56] O'Malley, J.P., "Communism and Fascism: The Reason They Are So Similar", *The Daily Beast*, https://www.thedailybeast.com/communism-and-fascism-the-reason-they-are-so-similar

He knew he would have a far better chance wining in the primaries as the Republican candidate and running against his good friend and Democrat candidate, Hilary Clinton. And he did. Therefore, when we examine the tenets of fascism, we can probably agree that Trump does not entirely fit that bill. However, Trump seemingly does reflect several of the bullet points previously shared as they pertain to the construct of fascism. And if I am being honest, I did not feel that I was living in a fascist society during the four years he was in office. My life carried on business as usual, for the most part until 2020. That is not to say, I did not feel a way about the children being separated from their family when taken by border security. Because I did. However, the caveat here is that this methodology of child separation is not anything brand new. Sadly, this activity has taken place under both Republican and Democrat administrations in the past. Moreover, we also must remember that under the Obama Administration, more undocumented immigrants were deported than under any other administration.

Yet, several Republican voters praise Trump for his efforts on improving the economy and has helped to reduce unemployment in the black community presumably. For example, according to 2018 Reuters article, "Trump is right, jobs for black Americans abound. Here's why it may not last", Howard Schneider asserts that "Trump often highlights that overall U.S. unemployment has reached a 50-year low on his watch, and that joblessness among black Americans has set a modern record as well. The unemployment rate for blacks sunk to 5.9 percent in May, the lowest since 1972 when the figure was first reported separately, but the milestone reflects a trend that took shape years before Trump took office. Black employment has risen about 1.3 million under Trump to hit a record 19.3 million in October, but job gains were the strongest during

Barack Obama's second term when recovery from the Great Recession became more firmly rooted. Recent data indicate job gains for blacks may already be leveling off."[57]

Similarly, according to 2020 economic article "Has Trump failed Black Americans?" in Brookings Rashawn Ray and Keon L. Gilbert, purport that "It is true that Black unemployment was at an all-time low in February 2020, before COVID-19. Yet, the Black unemployment rate under the Obama-Biden administration had one of the largest declines in American history following The Great Recession. Trump largely inherited a growing economy. However, when we look at the jobs picture, in addition to the unemployment rate, we are concerned about the quality of those jobs. Quality jobs pay living wages and benefits. Blacks still continue to be concentrated in lower sector jobs, which do not have adequate healthcare or paid sick leave and have disproportionately exposed them to COVID-19. For Black men, job prospects are even more limited. In addition to facing more barriers to work entry, the available jobs often do not provide enough money for them to provide financially for their families. For these men, the labor market has failed them. Thus, their unemployment is not factored into the rate. In fact, research notes that 1.5 million Black men are missing from social and economic life.

Trump's recent Platinum Plan claims to increase investments in Black communities by creating Black-small businesses and jobs. Despite the rapper Ice Cube's contributions, for some it is too little, too late. The

---

[57] Schneider, Howard, "Trump is right, jobs for black Americans abound. Here's why it may not last", *Reuters*, https://www.reuters.com/article/us-world-work-minority-employment-insigh/trump-is-right-jobs-for-black-americans-abound-heres-why-it-may-not-last-idUSKCN1NV0CM

Pay Protection Plan (PPP) from the Small Business Administration left Black businesses out in the cold. Over 90% of Black-owned small businesses that applied for PPP funding were denied. This has led to over 40% of Black-owned small businesses being shuttered during COVID-19. These realities document a callousness towards Black business owners who already have difficulties securing loans for development, and if provided a loan, are more likely to be offered one at higher interest rates than similar white-owned businesses would obtain, thereby increasing their operating costs. If achieving racial equity were actually part of Trump's agenda, the distribution of resources from the PPP would have explicitly included Black-and-other-minority-owned small businesses and would have allowed them to receive an equitable share."[58]

Additionally, when Trump touted about how much "he" has down for Black Americans, one might argue, as I did once, that his efforts are not efforts of a "fascist" and a "racist." Because no true to form fascist would help to close the unemployment gap in the black community, nor work to create more jobs to put more black Americans to work. And though Trump inherited the black unemployment rebound mantel from the Obama administration, under the Trump administration some improvements were made. Though Trump cannot take full credit for the improvement. The work was in progress long before the Trump administration. Nevertheless, Trump himself makes claims that he has helped improve the lives of many black people in this country. He spends time with members of the black caucus. He endorses people like

---

[58] Ray, Rashawn and Keon L. Gilbert, "Has Trump failed Black Americans?", *Brookings*, https://www.brookings.edu/blog/how-we-rise/2020/10/15/has-trump-failed-black-americans/

Diamond and Silk. He spends time in various black churches. He makes deals with various black leaders of their communities to help bring back jobs in distressed neighborhoods. And yet, Trump continually comes up short in many respects. But these acts garnered enough fan fair from some members of the black community which found Trump to be a man for the "people", whatever that means.

Therefore, when we consider the meaning of what a fascist is, we cannot entirely place Trump in that box. His actions, though self-serving on many levels, are not actions of a fascist. They may be actions of a narcissist. But the two are not the same thing. In sum, I think that people will adhere to a set of beliefs based on what they "feel", "think", and "believe" based on what they see in the news, read in the newspapers, and or create in their own minds as a personal and unique political construct which supports a set of political beliefs of either one person or one administration or both. On the surface, for some people, Trump is a fascist. For others, Trump is a patriot. For some people, Trump is a dictator. While for others, Trump is a hero. Do you see the polarities dancing in effortlessly in a beautiful tango together? The psychosocial construct of fascism in this instance is largely prompted by one's own political beliefs both individually and collectively.

Chapter 11
The Construct of Socialism

These days the argument from the farther right of the Republican spectrum, is the argument that the "left" is pushing for socialism in this country. The claim that is additionally made from some members of the farther right, perhaps Trumpian faction of the Republican party is that Democrats are socialists. But what is happening with this claim and the argument, is that they both are generalizing over seventy billion people who voted for Biden and Harris. Which in the minds of those individuals, anyone who voted for Biden and Harris are "socialists" and "communists." I find these sorts of statements to be extremely far-fetched and far-reaching. However, that is not to say that there are not socialists and communists which exist within the Democrat party. Just like we can agree that are neo-Nazi's and fascists which exist within the Republican party. There will always be these far-right and far-left factions. That does not mean, that people, generally speaking, by and large, who go to work every day, have families, who own homes, pay taxes, take family trips, and are law abiding members of society, are socialists and or communists. That belief would be like the belief held by some people within the Democrat party, that "all" Republicans are racists, sexist, xenophobic, fascists.

These gross generalizations have been damaging to say the least. And I hear these gross generalizations being made in different social settings as well as on the news, in television programs, movies, and shows. This "negative generalist thinking" is cyclical, perpetual and based on variety of skewed perceptions, planted in the minds of many individuals who subscribe to their own political beliefs and constructs. And when I say "planted" in the minds, I mean that these perceptions came from somewhere. However, in many cases, these perceptions come from a person, or a group of people, or an event, or an outcome, or an organization, or by news anchors repeating the same message repeatedly. This is how "psychological programming" takes place; through repetition of a statement, a phrase, a slogan, rhetoric that resonates with people, like mantras. In some cases, much of the perceptions formed, in my humble opinion are formed through "problem-solution-scenario's", when a person or group of people create a problem, thereby placing this person or group in a position to present their "solution" to the problem.

Moreover, "problem-solution-scenario" methodologies are not new. This way of thinking has been in existence for a very long time. Some might argue that "problem-solution-scenario" thinking is rooted in conspiracy theorizing. Perhaps on some level that kind of thinking, could be a form of conspiracy theorizing. And may also subscribe to some measure of political paranoia. However, circling back, some people choose to fall down a number of "rabbit holes" in their quest for searching for the truth. This is typically done from the comfort of one's own home using a computer as the means of digging for some "truth." But I ask, who's truth? Or truth according to whom? Truth is subjective these days. Because, what rings true for one person may not ring true for another. And by now you may be asking what does any of this have to do with the construct of socialism? When members of society claim that other members of society are "socialists" because of how they voted, or who they voted for, we find ourselves in very turbulent waters. The assumptions which are made by some people about other people based on their political subscriptions and beliefs helps absolutely no one in the grander scheme of things. And to suggest that more than half of the people who voted in the 2020 election are socialists, who want to take away people's freedoms, gun rights, brain wash children in the education system, who are responsible for pedophilia, human trafficking, is abhorrent. I do not understand that kind of thinking at all.

People, regardless of political affiliations do bad things. There are some people on the world who do engage with pedophilia, who are trafficking humans, who are hurting children, who are trying to whitewash history and or expose children to various lifestyles of other adults that I think is too much for a young person to be exposed to seeing, such as "drag queen reading time" as an example. I think that activity should be reserved for the parents to decide not an educational institution. Similarly, an educational institution should be teaching the truth to a degree about the origin story of this country, not painting Christopher Columbus in the light of a hero who found America when that is not accurate information at all. In fact, the origins of our education system came from white Anglo-Saxons, Protestants, Baptists, and other Christian faith factions. Our education system was not set up by "socialists." They were set up by white puritans, with their white ideas and white beliefs in their own level of superiority. When children saluted the flag and had prayer in public schools. In sum, our education system was about the indoctrination of other white children believing several lies about how this country came to be, about slaves, about black and brown people, about Native Americans and women.

Overtime, however, the basis of the education system changed in this country from being completely conservative to more liberal. And the current debate in the news and on social media is about whether schools should teach about "critical race theory." Regardless of opinions about what our education system is or was, the "brain washing" aspect, is one of the many claims made by some farther right Republican members of society who believe that all Democrats are socialists. Yet, to better understand, for the sake of clarity and continuity, lets us review what the term "socialist" or "socialism" means. According to Investopedia, "Socialism is a populist economic and political system based on public ownership (also known as collective or common ownership) of the means of production. Those means include the machinery, tools, and factories used to produce goods that aim to directly satisfy human needs. Communism and socialism are umbrella terms referring to two left-wing schools of economic thought; both oppose capitalism, but socialism predates the Communist Manifesto, a 1848 pamphlet by Karl Marx and Friedrich Engels, by a few decades.

In a purely socialist system, all legal production and distribution decisions are made by the government, and individuals rely on the state for everything from food to healthcare. The government determines the output and pricing levels of these goods and services.

Socialists contend that shared ownership of resources and central planning provide a more equal distribution of goods and services and a more equitable society.

KEY TAKEAWAYS

- Socialism is an economic and political system based on public ownership of the means of production.

- All legal production and distribution decisions are made by the government in a socialist system. The government determines all output and pricing levels.

- Citizens in a socialist society rely on the government for everything, from food to healthcare.

- Proponents of socialism believe that it leads to a more equal distribution of goods and services and a more equitable society.

- Examples of socialist countries include the Soviet Union, Cuba, China, and Venezuela.

- Socialist ideals include production for use, rather than for profit; an equitable distribution of wealth and material resources among all people; no more competitive buying and selling in the market; and free access to goods and services.

- Capitalism, with its belief in private ownership and the goal to maximize profits, stands in contrast to socialism.

- While socialism and capitalism seem diametrically opposed, most capitalist economies today have some socialist aspects."[59]

Moreover, "while socialism and capitalism seem diametrically opposed, most capitalist economies today have some socialist aspects. Elements of a market economy and a socialist economy can be combined into a mixed economy. And in fact, most modern countries operate with a mixed economic system; government and private individuals both influence production and distribution. Economist and social theorist Hans Herman Hoppe wrote that there are only two archetypes in economic affairs—socialism and capitalism—and that every real system is a combination of these archetypes. But because of the archetypes' differences, there is an inherent challenge in the philosophy of a mixed economy and it becomes a never-ending balancing act between predictable obedience to the state and the unpredictable consequences of individual behavior."[60]

---

[59] "Socialism", *Investopedia*, https://www.investopedia.com/terms/s/socialism.asp
[60] "Socialism", *Investopedia*, https://www.investopedia.com/terms/s/socialism.asp

Our country is currently a "mixed economy" and has been a mixed economy since the Great Depression which left millions of Americans without jobs, the elderly and single mothers with children were without assistance, children were homeless, there were food shortages and food riots, homeless families were living in parks and the level of desperation from fathers and husbands at that time was palpable. It was clear, something had to be done to remedy this national crisis. For example, according an article in the Constitutional Rights Foundation, "President Franklin D. Roosevelt focused mainly on creating jobs for the masses of unemployed workers, he also backed the idea of federal aid for poor children and other dependent persons. By 1935, a national welfare system had been established for the first time in American history. The emphasis during the first two years of President Franklin Roosevelt's "New Deal" was to provide work relief for the millions of unemployed Americans. Federal money flowed to the states to pay for public works projects, which employed the jobless. Some federal aid also directly assisted needy victims of the Depression. The states, however, remained mainly responsible for taking care of the so-called "unemployables" (widows, poor children, the elderly poor, and the disabled). But states and private charities, too, were unable to keep up the support of these people at a time when tax collections and personal giving were declining steeply."[61]

Additionally, "This is how welfare began as a federal government responsibility. Roosevelt and the members of Congress who wrote the welfare provisions into the Social Security Act thought that the need for federal aid to dependent children and poor old people would

---

[61] *Constitutional Rights Foundation*, https://www.crf-usa.org/bill-of-rights-in-action/bria-14-3-a-how-welfare-began-in-the-united-states.html

gradually wither away as employment improved and those over 65 began to collect Social Security pensions. But many Americans, such as farm laborers and domestic servants, were never included in the Social Security old-age retirement program. Also, since 1935, increasing divorce and father desertion rates have dramatically multiplied the number of poor single mothers with dependent children. Since the Great Depression, the national welfare system expanded both in coverage and federal regulations. From its inception, the system drew critics. Some complained that the system did not do enough to get people to work. Others simply believed the federal government should not administer a welfare system. As the system grew, so did criticism of it, especially in the 1980s and '90s. In 1992, candidate Bill Clinton, a Democrat, ran for president promising to "end welfare as we know it." In 1996, a Republican Congress passed and President Clinton signed a reform law that returned most control of welfare back to the states, thus ending 61 years of federal responsibility."[62]

As it stands, we have over eighty Federal Welfare programs in place ranging from Family Planning to Indian Human Services, from Social Security to Federal Pell Grants, for which I benefit from being in college. I have also benefited from state health insurance and food assistance. I also currently benefit from the Federal Supplemental Educational Opportunity Grant, and Pennsylvania Higher Education Assistance Agency (PHEAA) and the CARES Act. "The Coronavirus Aid, Relief, and Economic Security Act, also known as the CARES Act, is a $2.2 trillion economic stimulus bill passed by the 116th U.S. Congress and signed into law by President Donald Trump on March 27,

---

[62] *Constitutional Rights Foundation*, https://www.crf-usa.org/bill-of-rights-in-action/bria-14-3-a-how-welfare-began-in-the-united-states.html

2020, in response to the economic fallout of the COVID-19 pandemic in the United States."[63] Even a Republican president signed into law a welfare program such as the CARES Act to help Americans in a time of need, just like FDR who was considered a socialist.

---

[63] "CARES Act", *Wikipedia*

Chapter 12
The Construct of Conservatism

For many years, I considered myself a "liberal" without understanding what that term meant. Similarly, I rejected "conservatism" without fully understanding what the construct of conservatism meant. What's more, these days, the battle between the constructs of liberalism and conservatism in the online space has become interestingly volatile and demeaning. But those who consider themselves ultra-conservative view ultra-liberals as the worst kind of human. Similarly, the ultra-liberal views the ultra-conservative as the worst kind of human, in some online circles. However, before we go any further, let us define the construct of conservatism to gain more clarity on some of the thought processes and ideologies which accompany this faction of the Republican party.

For instance, according to Britannica, "Conservatism, is a political doctrine that emphasizes the value of traditional institutions and practices. Conservatism is a preference for the historically inherited rather than the abstract and ideal. This preference has traditionally rested on an organic conception of society—that is, on the belief that society is not merely a loose collection of individuals but a living organism comprising closely connected, interdependent members. Conservatives thus favour institutions and practices that have evolved gradually and are manifestations of continuity and stability. Government's responsibility is to be the servant, not the master, of existing ways of life, and politicians must therefore resist the temptation to transform society and politics. This suspicion of government activism distinguishes conservatism not only from radical forms of political thought but also from liberalism, which is a modernizing, anti-traditionalist movement dedicated to correcting the evils and abuses resulting from the misuse of social and political power."[64]

Moreover, the construct of conservatism is a political philosophy, "based on tradition and social stability, stressing established institutions, and preferring gradual development to abrupt change."[65] At first glance, this political philosophy seems reasonable. The caveat is to question "whose" traditions, by "whose" standards of social stability, and what established institutions according to "whose" recommendations? Looking back, during this country's developmental stages, conservatism was the measuring stick used to calculate governmental and societal growth spurts. Our founding fathers were themselves, conservatives. Many of the people which immigrated here from England were conservatives. The countries established institutions were conservative. Moreover, as societies formulated, traditions and social stability were both conservative. The level of patriotism elevated during the Revolutionary War and every other subsequent war, including World War II. One could argue that this country was a most conservative, nationalistic and patriotic country from the beginning, rooted deeply in the long-established Empire of Great Britain.

These conservative customs were not plucked from thin air. They were cultivated by years of personal and societal experience stemming from another country entirely. The construct of Conservatism did not exist in North America. Native American traditions were the traditions and societal standards in which tribal members adhered to. In fact, every political philosophy that we know was imported. They each

[64] "Conservatism", *Britannica*, https://www.britannica.com/topic/conservatism
[65] "Conservatism", *Merriam-Webster Dictionary*, https://www.merriam-webster.com/dictionary/conservatism

came from Europe and evolved over time to mean a myriad of different things. Now, the construct of Conservatism means something very different to those who have settled on the political plantations of left-leaning ideologies. Similarly, the construct of Liberalism means something very different to those who have settled on the political plantations of right-leaning ideologies. Because political culture began changing during the 1960s, the meanings of these two constructs have shape shifted to mean, in some regard, its opposite definition. What's more, societal norms and cultural norms changed during the 1960s, and therefore the political landscaped ultimately and most permanently resembled something different.

It was during this critical time in our history when the nature of politics morphed due to enormous cultural pressure applied by those who felt the pains of social injustices, discrimination, poverty, police brutality, racism on multiple fronts, educational, medical, financial, etcetera, in addition to segregation in the south. With all of these things happening, the politicians who ran for office who took a stance on these matters represented not the Conservative construct but the Liberal construct, the Democrat construct, rather than the Republican construct. Therefore, the largest voting block, the black community, in large part identified with policies which favored equality and equal justice initiated by Democrat president John F. Kennedy. This is where the tide turned for many black and brown people, for women, for the anyone who felt they were left in the cracks of society, perpetually overlooked and not considered in the grander scheme of policy making, and in legislation. In some online discussions, some argue that political parties changed their platforms in the 60s. And on some level, they did. However, what began to shift was not exactly political platforms but the players themselves.

I like to think of these two distinct political parties, Republican and Democrat, as parties which were hijacked by other groups, other traditionalists, extremists if you will, that sullied the basic nature of each, perverting the rudimentary nature of each and therefore, churning out an entirely different brand of each. This new brand of conservatism for example, became apparent and visible when people voted for Ronald Regan. Ronald Regan represented the essential tenants of conservatism ideology and philosophy which were attractive to many Republican voters. Add religion to the equation, such as with the evangelicals which supported Ronald Regan. In sum, the wealthy, the elite, the evangelical community, the traditionalists, and rural communities supported Ronald Regan. Moreover, those who voted for Regan felt that the "Regan Years" were the best years of this country. Some believe the at the Regan era was the most prosperous era this country had experienced.

Naturally, of course, with every perceived upside, there is a distinct and perceived downside. Many of the alleged conservative values did not include a number of other members of society, such as the mentally ill, the poor, black and brown people, the gay community as it were, women, generally speaking, the non-Christians, and others on the fringe of society. With these groups of people in mind, conservatism was not a perfect fit in many regards. Yet, the role of conservatism has evolved in some ways to include all members of society, yet maintaining some measurable distance between itself and those who do not align with its value system. Because the truth is, one could argue that the construct of conservatism essentially derived from the alleged moral code brought forth by the Ten Commandments. Meaning, that our white, slave owning "founding fathers" subscribed to the Christian ideology, Christian moral code, and Christian belief system in general. Protestants, Quakers, Presbyterians, Lutherans, Unitarians, and Anglicans, who in fact immigrated to the America's from Great Britain, and Europe in general, created a political identity rooted in Christian ethics and principles. Which is the foundation of our alleged democracy as we know it.

Hence, when some folks argue that this country is a Christian country, on some core levels in terms of it's "founding", they are not entirely wrong. However, the key take away here is that, these people who directly fled from one country to practice their form of religion freely, seemingly made their brand religion the focal point of American politics. As a result of Christian-like beliefs, the construct of Conservatism became the philosophy and the embodiment of American politics as a whole. However, even in the timeline of this construct, Conservatism began to take on a new face, a new form of expression, one in which protected the right to own slaves, and protected a particular way of life, primarily felt in the south, with some northern territories sprinkled in such as Virginia and Maryland.

However, it was the Civil War that defined a clear split in Conservative ideologies, dividing the ideological point of view held by the North and held by the South. With this in mind, one could argue that a "new Conservative" political landscape cultivated by southern states was created, and supported by wealthy landowners, who's wealth had been built up over generations, generating its own kind of political power and persuasion, the North had to contend with. But these polarizing ideological views engaged in conflict, claiming the lives of thousands of soldiers, and ending with the end of slavery, represented by the thirteenth amendment; white Dixiecrats, Klansmen, segregationists, and the like, held to their core conservative political beliefs and ideologies, regardless of constitutional amendments and states rights changes. Generations past, descendants of the so-called "Old Guard" also known as "Dixiecrats", Klansmen, segregationists and the like, have taken up the mantel and become politically affiliated to the point of holing positions of power, serving as Congressmen, Senators, Governors, Mayors, Councilmen, City Officials, Judges, Sherifs, Police Chiefs, and more.

With every passing decade and every passing presidential election, political identities continued to shape shift, therefore, rebranding and marketing the newest version and incarnation of Conservatism and the Conservative Party. And this newest incarnation of the Conservative Party, more commonly known as the Republican Party, has been yet again redefined by former President Donald J. Trump. The current identity crisis in which the Republican Party is undergoing is a result of the election of Donald J. Trump in 2016. Interestingly, this one human being, single handedly changed the face of American politics as we now know it. Furthermore, Trump became the face of the Republican Party and is responsible for the political makeover in which the Republican Party/ Conservative Party continues to undergo.

This new face of Conservatism resembles that of the original face of Conservatism, reflecting the alleged Christian moral codes and ethics. However, if one is looking more closely, Trump is the proverbial wolf in sheep's clothing, promoting himself as this alleged political savior of the working class, rural residents, and the patriots of this country. This man has been branded a hero by those who support him and support distortions and delusions of grandeur. Because when you look closely, you may be able to see the lies parading as truth, lies hidden behind a narrative and rhetoric spouted by Trump ensnaring those who believe this human being has their best interests at heart, and while playing the pawn in the political Ponzi scheme he continues to operate.

Chapter 13

The Construct of Liberalism

We have heard over a number of years Republicans refer to "liberals" as "leftists", "communists", "socialists", "Marxists" and "the radical left." Hence, branding has much to do with any political ideology and narrative. And these terms are not brand new. Additionally, these terms regarding Liberals within the Democrat Party had been used repeatedly by those who are on the side of white Christian or puritanical beliefs steeped in Nationalistic attitudes and superiority. Moreover, the previously mentioned terms are not entirely interchangeable, as they each mean something slightly different and are nuanced. However, for the sake of this chapter, we will focus on the construct of liberalism as we know it today. Of course, learning about its roots, will offer context, juxtaposed to the current incarnation of what Liberalism means to us today.

For example, in the 2014 article "The Origin of 'Liberalism'" in The Atlantic, Daniel B. Klein asserts that "up to 1769 the word was used only in pre-political ways, but in and around 1769 such terms as "liberal policy," "liberal plan," "liberal system," "liberal views," "liberal ideas," and "liberal principles" begin sprouting like flowers."[66] Moreover, the term liberal, according to the article means "allowing every man to pursue his own interest his own way, upon the liberal plan of equality, liberty and justice."[67] Which, in it's early days, makes complete sense. Currently, I still believe that the term "liberal" means exactly that. However, the politicization of that term has contorted the meaning to

[66] Klein, Daniel B. "The Origin of 'Liberalism'." The Atlantic, 2014, https://www.theatlantic.com/politics/archive/2014/02/the-origin-of-liberalism/283780/
[67] Klein, Daniel B. "The Origin of 'Liberalism'." The Atlantic, 2014, https://www.theatlantic.com/politics/archive/2014/02/the-origin-of-liberalism/283780/

understate something all together unrecognizable since being cast in a demonizing light by the far-right Republican's to support their narrative on the political stage. Additionally, the term "liberal" was originated not by the British Empire but by Scottish hierarchy in pursuit of liberty, equality and economic trade. From an economical perspective the term "liberal" represented the characteristics of trade agreements with other countries. So it's original format was not necessarily political but economic.

Fast forward, "in the 1820s the suffix "-ism" was attached to create "liberalism." And later in the century the Liberal Party rose in British politics."[68] What's more, Klein references an excerpt from the author Jonathan Parry. For example, "in his book The Rise and Fall of Liberal Government in Victorian Britain, Jonathan Parry writes, "Politicians were faced with the need to respond to the mass electorate, and they compromised accordingly … Liberals were committed to using the powers of central and local government pragmatically and constructively, so as to secure order, economy, free-market conditions and self-improvement." It was especially after 1880 that the Smithian sense of "liberal" began to lose traction to other, often contrary, meanings. The principal presumption of today's "liberalism" often lies with the status quo, or even with the idea that the government should "do something" to solve perceived problems."[69] The key words to consider are "perceived problems." Currently, from a socioeconomic perspective,

---

[68] Klein, Daniel B. "The Origin of 'Liberalism'." *The Atlantic*, 2014, https://www.theatlantic.com/politics/archive/2014/02/the-origin-of-liberalism/283780/
[69] Klein, Daniel B. "The Origin of 'Liberalism'." *The Atlantic*, 2014, https://www.theatlantic.com/politics/archive/2014/02/the-origin-of-liberalism/283780/

there are a number of problems, starting with lack of affordable housing, lack of affordable health care, lack of job opportunities in lower income areas, poverty, homelessness, you name it. These are not "perceived problems." These issues are real and require governmental support and help. And that is where the demonization begins by some Conservatives, specifically by Trumplicans.

The particular rhetoric spouted by the right is centered on the complaint that "liberals" want too much government involvement, which runs counter to the Republican political thought centered on small government and less government regulations. Whereas, the Democrat party for instance, and it's liberal members desire to have more government regulations and have more governmental involvement that essentially support the most vulnerable members of society such as black and brown folks, LGBTQIA+ members of society, the elderly, the unwell, homeless, children, undocumented immigrants, the poor, ex-military, and other marginalized community members of our society. In my humble opinion, I do not see such government involvement to be a negative given how poorly big corporations, the wealthy elite, state governments, our judicial system, police authorities, and other such organized entities, have treated it's workers, the poor, the vulnerable, and of course, the environment, generally speaking. Because individuals cannot rely on large corporations to essentially do the right thing, protesting for more government oversight is necessary. And that government oversight to protect vulnerable members of our society and our environment is the very ideal in which many liberals if not all liberals, strive to encourage within its own political party.

Conversely, some members of the Republican Party push for less regulation, which means more dumping of toxic waste into water ways, for example, or more dumping toxic waste into the soil and ground water creating health hazards for residents nearby. Moreover, less regulation means more money insurance companies get to pocket when folks have to elect to have a surgical procedure done, or when insurance companies increase monthly premiums simply because they can. Hence, this deregulatory attitude puts those who cannot afford to protect themselves against high medical bills, monthly premiums, poor drinking water, hazardous chemicals, toxic air, pollution, and so forth, in a very precarious position, which warrants more government involvement and more regulations. Additionally, legislating for gun control is another government involved action which needs to be taken given the amount of people who die each year by the illegal purchase of handguns and by assault rifles purchased by people under the age of 18 and lack of background checks. Because the truth is, the process to obtain a passport or driver's license is more arduous than is the process to purchase a firearm in this country. I find that to be serious problem and a poor prioritization of priorities which ultimately hurts the American people of this country.

When we closely examine the basic construct and political philosophy of liberalism, liberalism at its core seeks balance. For instance, the Wikipedia defines Liberalism as "a political and moral philosophy based on the rights of the individual, liberty, consent of the governed, political equality and equality before the law." That definition seems rather straightforward. However, some might argue, who tend to lean further to right of the political spectrum, that liberalism, as previously mentioned, is synonymous with communism, which does not compute. In the face of Conservatism, which tends to focus its efforts on traditional normative views steeped in Christian ideology, in large part, and moral attitudes to govern the masses, Liberalism challenges these normative views directly and unapologetically. Liberalism, the way I see it, is the yang to the Conservatisms yin. One in essence cannot exist without the other. Conservatism and Liberalism are political siblings which rival each other more often than they should or ought perhaps. But exist as each other's counterpart.

Even with this knowledge, liberalism, when only taking into consideration its essence, (liberal), or to "liberate", someone or something, is the very backbone of this political ideology. Further looking at the prefix of the term liberal (liber), we can draw upon a few other additional words that tie into this construct, such as liberty, liberation, liberators, and so on. All of these words pain a picture about the philosophy in totality. However, let us look more into the meaning of liberalism as definite by Encyclopedia Britannica. For instance, "liberalism, political doctrine that takes protecting and enhancing the freedom of the individual to be the central problem of politics. Liberals typically believe that government is necessary to protect individuals from being harmed by others, but they also recognize that government itself can pose a threat to liberty. As the American Revolutionary pamphleteer Thomas Paine expressed it in Common Sense (1776), government is at best "a necessary evil." Laws, judges, and police are needed to secure the individual's life and liberty, but their coercive power may also be turned against the individual. The problem, then, is to devise a system that gives government the power necessary to protect individual liberty but also prevents those who govern from abusing that power."[70]

The con, in this case, is an abuse of power, in which government is in control of everything and of everyone, which can be perceived as "communism" by many Republican voters and right leaning non-voters.

---

[70] "Liberalism." *Britannica.* https://www.britannica.com/topic/liberalism

Because as we already know, governments in control over the people are communistic countries such as Russia and China, for examples. And perception is a funny thing. In a very real way, perception is reality. Which means that if a number of people who are Republican voters, or right leaning non-voters, perceive this country as becoming a communist country because of things like mask mandates, COVID vaccinations, providing housing for the unhoused, fast tracking immigration to allow people fleeing for their lives access to the United States, then that is what it looks like to them. And these perceptions are what will continue to push the Conservative agenda further along, virtually steam rolling over the concerns of many members of our society, black and brown communities and people in urban environments, the poor, the sick, the elderly, children, the homeless, immigrants, women, transgender, individuals and those who suffer from addiction. Without proper governmental oversight to protect a large swath of the American public, rights and liberties will continue to evaporate.

Conversely, too much governmental involvement can create an imbalance in power, which can be a much larger problem if not kept in check. Too much government oversight, are what the framers were worried about. Which is completely understandable. Although, one could argue that when the pendulum has swung the other direction, to the furthest reaches of the right, people like Governor Ron DeSantis who is presently working to ban books, outlaw reproductive rights, and gender affirming care in the state of Florida, our country could become fascist. In fact, when we look at what is taking place in states like Florida and Texas, these legislatures and policies passed are reflective of the same kind of laws established and subsequently enforced by the Nazis. And with the 2024 election around the corner, fascism too, is right around the corner, if you consider the fact that DeSantis intends to use his experience of changing Florida State Laws, to change the country at large. Which would be disastrous. Liberalism and what it stands for, could be run into the ground by Conservatives, religious zealots, and Neo Nazis. Democracy as we know it would end. And we would be thrust into the 18th century on many levels.

Chapter 14

The Construct of Corporatism

At the center of political debates is the construct of corporatism. In other words, one could argue that our country is not democracy but a corporatocracy. That our country is run by corporate billionaires and that their interests supersede that of the people. And in large part, that is the case. For example, with regard to big oil, big Pharma, big agriculture, big sugar, big so on and so forth, those that lobby for these kinds of corporate entities do so at the behest of board members, shareholders, executives, and chief executive officers. Keeping in mind that when legislation passes some new bill, or new law or legality, these corporations are considered greatly. Moreover, when we think about how various administrations offer tax incentives, cuts and so forth, these gifts are not gifts bestowed upon the people but bestowed upon the wealthy. In the meantime, the average citizen of this country has to pay their "fair share" of taxes, even if that comes at the cost of one's ability to keep a roof over their heads, food to eat and the utilities on. In other words, with corporate entities and their interests controlling the political scheme of things, the rest of us have to live with whatever choices are made and or suffer the consequences of their actions.

Not only that, the environment takes a substantial hit, as well as lower income communities, black and brown communities, rural communities with little to no access to medical care. When a corporation selects a location to house their toxic chemical plant for example, it cannot do so without the law being on their side. That means, when pockets are presumably lined, the right law makers pass laws to allow those corporations to set up shop in the backyard of lower income communities, vulnerable communities, communities without proper legal representation or the means to acquire legal representation. Thus, the corporation can conduct their business and dump their toxic chemicals into the surrounding area, polluting the soil and groundwater of nearby communities, and animal habitats. There is seemingly no end to the corruption. Which is why, as citizens of this country, we must take responsibility for our level of complacency and change the trajectory of our thought process when we elect certain officials into office, so as to not continue repeating a destructive trend.

The problem, however, is that some folks have forgotten who stands to gain the most when Republican voters vote for people who care more about their political donations, campaign donations, contributions, and stock investments, than they do about regular every day working people. In other words, in large part, Republican voters continually vote against their own interests. In particular, Republican voters, who do not have access to medical care, the ones who keep losing crops to climate change, the ones who are unable to get a job due to lack of education, or who lack affordable housing, vote against their own interests. These specific Republican voters who believe, for example, that Donald Trump will save them from their despair, have lost touch with the simple fact that while they send him their money, he gets to eat well, live in a handful of really nice homes, fly around in his private jet, and visit different cities complaining that he's the victim. I find this entire way of thinking on the part of the poor Republican voter deranged in many respects. But it's not their fault entirely. Corporations and other business entities are at the helm of this illusion, benefiting from those who cannot see past their own noses.

But this is not anything new. Businessmen and corporate entities have been shaping this country since its founding. Think about the background of those who signed the United States Constitution, for example. Not only did these men own slaves, but they owned land, they were bankers, inventors, physicians, manufacturers, shippers, financiers, engineers, and were the wealthiest of people of the Colonies. These men owned property, had investments, made deals, owned high yielding plantations, and had thriving businesses. They had the means and the influence to shape this country in their image and did so that helped to benefit them and line their pockets. In other words, there was no true altruism here. Perhaps quakers such as William Penn, the founder of the Colony of Philadelphia, was a bit more altruistic than other framers of this country. Though some might like to believe that each of these men were noble and had the interests of the people in mind when they announced the separation from the Crown on July 2nd, 1776. Followed by the adoption of the Declaration of Independence on July 4th, 1776. However, generally speaking by and large, the decision made to do so was not about the people of this land, because slaves were not considered, Native Americans were not considered, women were not considered, the poor were not considered, nor were the sick, nor the military for that matter.

Corporations thus, stayed in power and gained more power with the help of free labor provided by African bodies, in south and the north. Tobacco, cotton, sugar and rice in some parts, were the most profitable agricultural crops during the seventeenth and eighteenth centuries. These businesses were able to weigh in on elections and support the candidates that would in turn support their businesses. Fast forward, not much as changed on that note. The only thing that may have changed is party affiliation. By stripping away Republican and Democrat ideologies and identities and looking closely at who stands to financially gain the most with certain political officials in power, we can surmise that our elected officials have, in large part, been influenced by the one percent. With this in mind, the argument that this country is not a real democracy but a corporatocracy, is not entirely inaccurate. We can also now add to the fold of the "big's" is Tech. Now that we are in the age of information, technology is as the center. And it too, has a vested interest in our political landscape and how it is shaped. Thus, they have lobbyists too, to argue on their behalf, against or for laws that will benefit them, regardless of how many "diverse" people they hire to look good in the eyes of the public.

With companies such as Meta, Amazon, Netflix, Twitter, Apple, etcetera, they now have skin in the game and need the law to be on their side so as to improve their bottom line does not detract from it. The billions of dollars they bring in annually, while staying on top of pieces of legislation that keep their interests afloat, keeps these corporate entities at the top of the corporate heap of control, power, and influence. Meanwhile, we pay our little $14.99 monthly subscriptions, complaining about the state of the world and our political bullshit, they are enjoying vacations in Bora Bora, flying into space in their own privately funded spaceships, and living the dream. You have to look at the hilarity of it all because you can't make this stuff up. Corporations and companies, as long as they exist, have an impact on our political system— which will be greatly influenced, and infiltrated by the mega wealthy. Though we are supposed to be a democratic society, a Republic, one could argue, that we are anything but.

Corporatocracy is at the center of our Democracy. Global trading, the World Monetary Fund, the International Banking System, and other forms of global interconnectedness rely heavily on each countries political landscape. In order for the cash to flow from one country to the next, governments have to be in alignment with one another for the most part. Each country Gross Domestic Product cannot swell without globalism. This new world order has been established since the beginning of civilizations. Of course, some of us act and behave as if globalism is brand new. It is not. The Egyptians have been in business with the Roman Empire and other countries for as long as it was in power. Similarly, the Roman Empire has been in business with other countries for as long as it has been in power. And so on and so forth. The British Empire had simply refined this way of life with colonizing a multitude of geographic locations around the world and forcing deals of trade with governmental heads and officials. And now the United States of America, along with other countries such as Canada, Britain, the United Arab Emirates, India, South America, China, Russia, and so on, stand to gain substantially through the financial artery of globalism.

Hence, with each countries governmental systems in place, ensuring certain party heads, and elected officials is paramount when it comes to global financial growth and gains. Politics and Corporations coexist and cannot exist independently of each other. In fact, one cannot survive without the other. They are interconnected, interwoven, interdependent on each other. The political arena was established by the wealthy not the poor. Political ideologies were put in place by the wealthy not the poor. Political parties were constructed by the wealthy not the poor. We have to remember that everything we have been programmed to accept is a lie. Nothing is as it seems. But we live in the delusion that our political system is for the support and the benefit of the people when, more or less, it is for the support and the benefit of corporate shareholders, Chief Financial Officers, board members, investors, and so on. Not for the rest of us. We all just work, pay our share of taxes, spend money, lose money, go into debt, try to save money, put into a 401k, or a Roth IRA, and hope that there is social security left to help us in our older years. But even that is a question mark.

Part Three—

Political Myopia

"With every passing generation there's a new political energy, spirit, essence, ideology and identity. If we cling to that which we generationally believe, we are inflexible and unwilling to create the much-needed space for new political perspectives. Thus, political myopia ensues. Therefore, with each generation, let us hope, one, among the many, chooses to break the cycle of stagnation and steer us into the new."

— The Unconventional Yogi

Political Science Essays...

Essay # 1

American culture is arguably one of the most expansive and ever evolving cultures on the planet. What's more, American culture does not subscribe to one singular ideology. Some would argue, as Steven Warshawsky, argues in his essay "What Does It mean to Be an American" in the book The Enduring Debate by David T. Canon, John J. Coleman and Kenneth R. Mayer, that to be American, is a "way of life". Warshawsky makes the distinction known to the reader that to be American does not constitute geographic location. However, by this logic, if being American is about a country and its people's alleged way of life, then if I lived in Canada, I would be adopting the Canadian "way of life", whatever that means for a Canadian, which I am not sure if adopting another country's "way of life" should mean I am "American" or "Canadian", as examples. I suppose, my issue is the distinction often made about our so-called way of life that is classified and characterized as being "American" is more superior than the way of life of those who live in another country.

I believe that as a citizen of this country, I cannot be so arrogant as to believe that the American way of life is superior, and all other ways of living are inferior. That would be a mistake to hold our country is such high regard as to discredit other countries and their way of living. Because the truth is, the American way of living is not as glorious as some may believe it to be in many respects. For instance, recent protests concerning the unjust killings of unarmed black men and women by the hands of white police officers, clearly illustrates a host of social injustices and issues which date as far back as the importation of Africans and the genocide committed against Native Americans. In other words, systemic racism continues to run unchecked to a large degree. With this in mind, if being American means tolerating the egregious and repetitive racist acts committed against black and brown people in this country, not to mention the insane conditions of various Indian Reservations in this country, bigotry, and more, I am not sure if I am thrilled to call myself American by Warshawksy's definition, if racism, bigotry, intolerance, and hate crimes are considered a "way of life". Conversely, I do not wish to live in the slums of Soweto either or in some part of the Republic of the Congo, where women and children are often abducted, raped and killed. The Congo or Soweto are not geographic areas I wish to live in.

I will say however, that to be American in my view, which fits within the trifecta of what Daniel J. Elazar illustrates in his essay "Three Political Cultures" in text The Enduring Debate, is to embrace the fundamental ideas of equality, tolerance, justice, liberty, freedom and the pursuit of happiness of which our Founding Fathers forged through the establishment of the Declaration of Independence, the Constitution of the United States, along with the Bill of Rights. These ideas or hopes, some may argue, dreams, are the stuff of courage, bravery, fortitude, a willingness to stand firmly in one's position to be treated fairly and justly in this country, to be counted as a citizen and to be considered an equal member of society, regardless of one's skin tone or ethnicity or gender or sexual preference or orientation, or religious affiliation or political affiliation, etcetera. What makes America great(ish), dare I even use the verbiage, is our individualism, moralism and traditionalism views, as Elazar denotes. Moreover, what makes this country stand out is our diverse nature, our multiculturalism, our evolving populace. The fact remains, our Founding Father's were immigrants. They were not native to these lands. In fact, those who fled from other countries to colonize this land mass, were immigrants. The only ones who are truly native to this land are the indigenous peoples of this land and their decedents. However, those who have either fled here, were forced to be slaves here, or who found it worth their time to set up colonies here, were immigrants and their offspring became natives to this country. Therefore, when there is a narrative that spins in a direction that opposes immigration, for example, and bolsters the idea of "Americanism", I shake my head in disappointment given the bloody and evil roots of how America came to be established in the first place.

What is most interesting is how splintered our country is in its beliefs and ideologies regarding what it means to be American. Warshawsky seems to think that being American means "adopting our way of life and loves this country above all others." Conversely, Warshawsky asserts that "today the danger is not armed rebellion, but the slow erasing of the American national character through a process of political and cultural redefinition." Some would agree with his sentiment, as some would argue that our country is slowing becoming a socialist country and or a communist country, which is utterly preposterous, because some are feeling the effects of this so-called "political and cultural redefinition". All that sounds like to me, is that some people are genuinely afraid of multiculturalism, as Warshawsky has expressed. There is a disconnect with that sort of belief and narrative. The disconnect is not recognizing the atrocities committed against black and brown people, native people, immigrants, women, farmers, soldiers, veterans, elderly, sick, homeless, and the poor. If redefining some cultural and political standards needs to take place in order for our country to be more inclusive to meeting the needs of every citizen while also supporting free market, the ability to progress, to build and create business and be successful, I am all for it. Change is needed. It is time. Leaning on the old, antiquated ideology of Americanism, is a slow drag on moving forward in a way that strengthens us as a diverse nation, not celebrates whiteness, white elitism, white superiority, and white men who founded this country that still owned slaves and held women as their own concubine against their will. This includes William Penn. He couldn't help himself either. When we as a country continue to embrace the ideals of men who deliberately considered black men as three fifths of a man, should be called into question at some level about the "soul" of this country as Biden has referred—to "win back the soul of this country." I am not even certain if I buy what he is selling either, but he has a point. The soul of this country is dark, and something must be done.

In conclusion, I am not exactly sure which values I think most distinctly define American culture today given its past and it's present. There is much to atone for. Reparations have yet to be made. There are still those in power who wish to keep those at the bottom while they remain at the top, who wish to do the bare minimum to keep things functioning and nothing more. However, moralistic political views seem to be present in some areas of the country, but individualism and traditionalism both seem to be more pronounced. However, in terms of political control, I think our country still subscribes to Ascriptive Americanism in many respects regarding "some" of our politicians and others who holds some sort of political office. Therefore, the fight over racial equality will continue. The struggle between the top one percent and the bottom ninety-nine percent will continue. The battle of gender equality and rights will continue. Finally, I hope that moralistic political views are the views politicians and those engaged in the political conversation and or debate embrace as a standard. In essence, that is the America I am waiting for. Hence, the fight for good over evil, for justice and equality, while preserving our rights and freedoms to express our concerns, ultimately underlines what can be defined as American culture based on the paradoxical political ideologies and identities.

Works Cited

Elazar, Daniel J. "The Three Political Cultures." Canon, David T., Kenneth R. Mayer and John J. Coleman. The Enduring Debate. New York: W. W. Norton & Company, 1997. 14-25.

Warshawsky, Steven. "What It Means to Be American." Canon, David T., Kenneth R. Mayer and John J. Coleman. n.d.

Essay #2

Summary: "The Power to Persuade," from
Presidential Power by Richard Neustadt

The essay "The Power to Persuade, from Presidential Power" written by Richard Neustadt, summarizes what presidential power is, how it is used, and in what ways presidential power of persuasion is exercised. For example, and according to Neustadt, it is worth noting that "the key to presidential power is the power to persuade—to convince others that they should comply with the president's wishes because doing so is in their interest. Presidents persuade by bargaining: making deals, reaching compromise positions; in other words, the give and take that is part of politics."[71] In sum and according to Neustadt, "persuasive power, thus defined, amounts to more than charm or reasoned argument…For the men, he would induce to what he wants done on their own responsibility will need or fear some acts by him on his responsibility." Neustadt neatly characterizes presidential power to persuade others as a "give and take" relationship. This give and take relationship woven into the fabric of presidential power of persuasion has evolved as a by-product of our governmental structure, a structure set in place by the framers of our Constitution. For instance, Neustadt states that "the constitutional convention of 1787 is supposed to have created a government of "separated powers." In effect, "it did nothing of the sort. Rather, it created a government of separated institutions sharing

---

[71] (Canon, Coleman, & Mayer, 1997)

powers."[72] Essentially, Neustadt discusses what these persuasive powers are, why these powers of persuasion matter, their effects and so on.

In this essay, Neustadt provides context regarding the shared powers between the Executive, Legislative and Judicial Branches of government, including "Cabinet officers, agency administrators, and military commanders" [73] Neustadt argues that "the essence of a President's persuasive task is to convince such men that what the White House wants of them is what they ought to do for their sake and on their authority." What's more, Neustadt references Eisenhower's belief in that a president "would not need no power other than the logic of his argument." Respectively, by this logic, one could agree that, in a more beautiful world, a less complicated world, where people in power would govern with their conscience rather than their ego, Eisenhower's sentiment is sound. However, Neustadt suggests that "the men who share in governing this country frequently appear to act as though they were in business for themselves." Moreover, given the historical timeline of almost every president and or administration, this ideology rings true, particularly so, with Trump and the Trump Administration and its alarming use of presidential powers of persuasion over Republican members of both Congress and the Senate. Conversely, can only hope that with perhaps our current administration and future administrations, one may use their powers of persuasion for doing "good" in the world, rather than to stoke fires of fear in members of Congress, the Senate, Representatives, Heads of various Government Agencies, etcetera, if favors are not given, or if loyalty is not given, or if the best deals are not made.

---

[72] (Neustadt, 1997)
[73] (Neustadt, 1997)

Works Cited

Canon, David T., John J. Coleman and Kenneth R. Mayer. The Enduring Debate. New York: W.W. Norton & Company, Inc., 1997., "The Power to Persuade," from Presidential Power" by Richard Neustadt.

Essay #3

Arugment in favor of or against a political third-party in the U.S.

Upon reading the piece "Ending the Presidential-Debate Duopoly" by Larry Diamond and "A Third Party Won't Fix What's Broken in American Politics" by Ezra Klein, I conclude that Larry Diamond makes a better argument for the case of ending the political duopoly in this country. However, Klein additionally highlights some key points as to why adding or at least trying to include a third-party may cause more problems than it can solve. Yet, based on a singular key fact, in which Diamond clearly illustrates, his argument is strengthened. For example, the singular fact Diamond purports has to do with the Commission of Presidential Debates. For instance, Diamond asserts that "two-thirds of Americans say they wish they had the option to vote for an independent candidate for president. But any alternative to the 162-year-old duopoly of Democrats and Republicans is blocked by the system the two parties have created." What's more, "the obstacle imposed by a crucial but little known and unaccountable gatekeeper, the Commission on Presidential Debates (CDP)." Diamond states that "members of this unelected and unaccountable commission have established a rule that makes it impossible for an independent, nonpartisan, or third-party ticket to gain access to the general election debates." Moreover, "in contemporary era these debates have become such a dominant focus on political attention that no candidate (and particularly not a third one) can become president without participating."

All of this to be said, it is evident to me that the duopoly created was intended to box all other possible contenders out leaving only enough room for Democrat and Republican candidates to compete for the Iron Throne, so to speak. I believe the duopoly to be failing system in much need of an overhaul. Furthermore, I believe that based on poor voter turnout, for example, may possibly support the notion that this decrepit duopoly is doomed to fail in the long run and therefore, to be so vested in its decrepitude is not worthwhile. However, Klein argues "a third-party won't fix what's broken in American politics" because a third-party essentially needs "some sort of unique agenda." Moreover, Klein asserts that "America's unaffiliated voters are moderates." Meaning, us unaffiliated voters are not aligned with Washington's elites, such as "Unity 08, or No Label, or Mike Bloomberg, or Simpson-Bowles." Instead, we are the kind of unaffiliated voters who are considered extremists, "blithely crosses left and right lines, then doubles back on itself again." Klein continues to argue his claim about how a third-party not being a solution stating that because "congress is driven by disagreement and" has "an inability to compromise", "a third-party would simply add another set of disagreements and another group who could potentially block action to the mix."

In conclusion, I do agree with the possibility of a third-party adding to some of the chaos in Congress. I also believe that even through the chaos, order and compromise can be made. Klein closes his argument stating that "it's hard to see, a third-party, "fixing the fact that Washington can't do much with the ideas it already does take seriously." Meaning, that Washington seems to be fixed in place and a third-party isn't going to move it in any profound direction as some of us might think or believe, which I do not think is entirely accurate. In the end,

Klein's perspective focused on disagreements in Congress and the unaffiliated voter was well argued but leaned towards opinions rather than facts. Whereas Diamond provided statistics, numbers and important information pertaining to the Commission on Presidential Debates, for example, to help support his position, which allowed me to better understand his argument. Between the writers, Diamond clearly stated his points, provided information to support his points, and provided an objective perspective about the pros and cons of a duopoly and a third-party. For these reasons, I believe Diamond made a better argument about the slow decline of the political duopoly. Yet, I do consider Klein's position regarding how a third-party may not necessarily be the solution to a long-standing problem.

Works Cited

Diamond, Larry. "Ending the Presidential-Debate Duopoly." Canon, David T., John J. Coleman and Kenneth R. Mayer. The Enduring Debate. New York: W.W Norton & Company, 1997. 385-387.

Klein, Ezra. "A Third Party Won't Fix What's Broken in American Politics." Canon, David T. , John J. Coleman and Kenneth R. Mayer. The Enduring Debate. New York: W.W. Norton & Company, 1997. 388-391.

Essay #4

"Beyond Tocqueville, Myrdal, and Hartz: The Multiple Traditions in America"

The essay by Roger Smith offers a back story about American politics with highlighting its conflicting political ideologies and traditions. However, what we as Americans must remember when we contemplate the origins of our story is, how did we get here. Not exactly the "here", in terms of a time and place, but the philosophical "here", as in political beliefs, values, traditions, feelings, moods, emotions, and thought processes. Being that this land was first inhabited by Native people, followed by Colonialism, followed by the illusory "American Dream", riddled with inequalities and privilege, it is no wonder that the political struggles continue even today. In the essay, "Beyond Tocqueville, Myrdal, and Hartz" The Multiple Traditions in America" by Smith, He asserts that "considerable success of the proponents of inequalitarian ideas reflects the power these traditions have long had in America." In sum, Smith illustrates that America is not rooted in one tradition but in seemingly three, two of which are congruent, while one runs counter and quintessentially conflicts with the foundational roots of life, liberty and the pursuit of happiness for all. For instance, Ascriptive Americanism, "an illiberal view of social hierarchy where some groups are on top and others are below" as Smith defines, the ideology of life, liberty and the pursuit of happiness is limited to only "some groups" and excludes all others.

To better understand what these traditions are it is worthwhile to know what they are, as Smith shares. For example, Smith defines "Liberal here refers to its original meaning from eighteenth century political and economic theory— a philosophy that focuses on the individual and minimizing government intervention in daily life. Within liberal tradition, the beliefs in equality, private property, liberty, individualism, protection of religious freedom, and democracy are especially powerful." Ascriptive Americanism on the other hand, believes this liberal view is only offered to "those on top are deemed to be deserving of the rights and benefits the liberal tradition can offer; those below are not." The third political view is that of Republicanism. Though Republicanism is not well defined in the essay, it should be noted that Republicanism is not the same as being Republican–the two are not one in the same. Republicanism in the case of this essay refers to a liberal ideology or view that "the liberty of a country's citizens is constantly being threatened by those in power, and it is the responsibility of those citizens to protect that power." (Encyclopedia Britannica) In other words, Republicanism is a liberal and equalitarian view and is essentially against dictatorships, monarchies–autocracies of any kind.

Smith exposes the narrow view of Tocqueville's view by shedding light on the fact that the political foundations of America were formulated by the white elite–white wealth–those in power. For example, Smith states that "for over 80% of U.S. history, its laws declared most of the world's population to be ineligible for full American citizenship solely because of their race, original nationality, or gender. For at least two-thirds of American history, the majority of the domestic adult population was also ineligible for full citizenship for the same reasons." Smith goes on to not that "the Tocquevillian story is thus deceptive because it is too narrow. It is centered on relationships among a minority of Americans (white men, largely of norther European ancestry) …derived from the hierarchy of political and economic statuses men have held in Europe; monarchs and aristocrats, commercial burghers, farmers, industrial and rural laborers and indigents." Simply put, the historical picture the Tocquevillian story portrays and that Smith challenges, is a picture of American politics from the minds of those in power, who could afford to make laws, who could afford to administer punishments and practices of enforcements to their laws, while the rest of the country struggled for equality, liberty and justice. And as long as these white elites of the eighteenth century maintained their control over the populace through laws, policies, rules, and ordinances, thus, to essentially maintain Ascriptive Americanism way of life, struggles would perpetually ensue. However, this is the point of this essay– to show how America is unique. Because it is through the various and continual struggles of people striving of equality, for liberty, for justices, and for the pursuit of happiness that sets this country apart from all other countries. Smith concludes by stating that "The achievements of Americans in building a more inclusive democracy certainly provide reasons to believe that illiberal forces will not prevail" and that "we must analyze America as the ongoing product of often conflicting multiple traditions." American Democracy in truth is an ideal–a living breathing–ever evolving ideal, that we the people give breath to through our efforts to demand equality, justice, truth and continue to strive towards both our collective and individual happiness.

Works Cited

Canon, David T., John J. Coleman and Kenneth R. Mayer. The Enduring Debate. New York: W.W. Norton & Company, Inc., 1997.

Encyclopedia Britannica. n.d.

Essay #5

Federalist, No. 15 and the new Constitution

Alexander Hamilton–one of the founding fathers and founder of the nation's financial system, wore many hats such as but limited to being a banker, statesman, legal scholar, military commander, lawyer and economist was played a key role in the ratification of the new Constitution through the "Federalist papers; originally written as a series of newspaper editorials intended to persuade New York to ratify the Constitution" which remains one of the "most valuable exposition of the political theory underlying the Constitution." (Canon, Coleman and Mayer) The Federalist Papers of which fifty-one out of eighty-five were written by Hamilton essentially added the necessary steam behind the motivation to ultimately ratify the Constitution, which pointed out the failures of the Articles of Confederation while at the same time noting the weaknesses exposed within the central government, which "lacked the ability to levy taxes and regulate commerce, issues that led to the Constitutional Convention in 1787 for the create of the new federal laws under the United States Constitution." (History) Prior to ratification, "Congress was given authority to make treaties and alliances, maintain armed forces and coin money." (History)

Hamilton's actions through the writing of the Federalist Papers brought awareness to the cracks of governance which was viewed as not very strong and demanded change in order to change the trajectory of its governmental path at the time. What's more, "in the Federalist, No. 15, Alexander Hamilton is at his best arguing for the necessity of a stronger central government than the established under the Articles of

Confederation. He points out the practical impossibility of engaging in concerted action when each of the thirteen states retains virtual sovereignty, and the need for a strong central government to hold the new country together politically and economically." (Canon, Coleman and Mayer) In Hamilton's plea he asserts that, "Congress at this time scarcely possess the means of keeping up the forms of administration till the states can have time to agree upon a more substantial substitute for the present shadow of federal government." The summation of Hamilton's writings coupled with the Continental Convention spawns a new Constitution, one in which provides our government with three branches of government, legislative, executive and judicial, from the former solitary legislative branch.

In conclusion, Hamilton's efforts certainly succeeded in ameliorating the concerns regarding the Articles of Confederation. Moreover, Hamilton's primary concerns were valid and justifiable given the political and economic weakened position in which the United States was in post American Revolutionary War and all of the debt accumulated through loans owed primarily to France. Because of inflation, the need to collect taxes were thematic but regarded as suggestive by most states, which then led to Shay's Rebellion of 1786-1787, "an armed uprising in Western Massachusetts and Worcester in response to a debt crisis among the citizenry and in opposition to the state governments increased efforts to collect taxes both individually and on their trades." (History). Ultimately, this rebellion was used as an example to support Hamilton's argument for a stronger government. Hamilton's closes his argument eloquently claiming that "the measures of the Union have not been executed; and the delinquencies of the states are step by step matured themselves to an extreme, which has, at length, arrested all of the wheels of national government and brought them to an awful stand." (Hamilton)

Works Cited

Canon, David T., John J. Coleman and T. Kenneth Mayer. The Enduring Debate. New York: W.W. Norton & Company, Inc., 1997.

Hamilton, Alexander. "The Federalist, No. 15." Canon, David T., John J. Coleman and Kenneth R. Mayer. The Enduring Debate. New York: W.W. Norton & Company, Inc., 1997. 54-58.

History. Articles of Confederation. 27 October 2009. October 2009. <https://www.history.com/topics/early-us/articles-of-confederation>.

Essay #6

The Decline of Collective Responsibility in American Politics

By Morris P. Fiorina

Since the 2016 election, I have made mention to a number of friends and family members, that I no longer believe in the two-party system as it were. I have groused about how a two-party system, such as the Democrat Party and the Republican Party. Though political parties and affiliations do also include Libertarian and Independents, the two largest party affiliations are Democrat and Republican, both of which I believe are crippling this country. My additional grouse had to do with feeling as though our political system or government, over the past twenty to thirty years, has shape shifted into what is coined as a "corporatocracy" in which our economic and political systems is controlled by corporations or corporate interests. Perhaps this has been the case for much longer. The possibility of our Government being resembling a corporatocracy, commingled with the long hard struggle of minorities and the marginalized, gives way to what Morris P. Fiorina writes about as "The Decline of Collective Responsibility in American Politics" in The Enduring Debate. Of course, there are a number of variables in which Fiorina conveys is the result of this decline. One more pronounced variable is concerned with distrust of the American political system as a whole and the need for an increasing need for "government to act positively" as Fiorina states.

Circling back to the two parties, which I believe no longer needs to remain as such, are backed by special interests and groups–heads of major industries such as Big Oil, Big Food, Big Pharma, etcetera which seem to dictate the political flow of our country to such an extent that even Michelle Obama herself had to back off her proposal of getting American's healthy through her "Let's Move" campaign launched in 2010, in an effort to combat childhood obesity and Obama's healthy school lunch program, as examples. Because the sugar industry was and still is a wildly profitable industry, Michelle Obama's "Let's Move Campaign" challenged this industry, which elicited a reaction. Thus, forcing the initiative to bend in such a way that Big Food was still able to pull the string necessary to remain a foot hole in American dietary realm. When this workaround was established by Big Food, I knew her campaign would be short lived and that young people would still be eating poorly, gaining weight and suffering a myriad of health problems. As it turns out, I was right. As the obesity rate has not declined in this country.

That being said, it is my belief that the collective responsibility that ought to be present is fading away very slowly, very gradually, not because it is the fault of the citizens, but because this disintegration is the fault of those politicians who enjoy getting their pockets lined. This includes electing the right president and the right senator and congressman/woman, the right house of representative, the right city council member, and so on. There is a general lack of trust in our political officials to act responsibly. However, Fiorina is attributing this decline to a weakening of the political parties as if having them would be a benefit in an effort to bolster collective responsibility or to revitalize it. I disagree with this notion due to the fact that much of our economic issues, issues concerning policing, education, health care, etcetera, are largely attributed to two parties playing tug of war with the citizens of this country for control and domination. I do not believe our political system is so fragile that after two hundred plus years, either side can't seem to figure things out and pull together. I do not believe that our so-called fragility is a result of a decline of collective responsibility. I believe it is in large part due to money. Since the dawn of the industrial revolution, industry is what created what we have now to this date. Add the technological "revolution" if you will to this mix and now we have a power couple, so strong that it shapes our ever decision both individually and collectively. From a political perspective, Fiorina is simply sharing what he, through his body of research and study and experience, believes are the core causes of this decline being centrally a lack of party loyalty in some regard, more or less and a lack of strong political ties and attachments by the populace.

For instance, Fiorina states that "the only way collective responsibility has ever existed, and can exist given our institutions, is through the agency of the political party; in American politics, responsibility requires cohesive parties." I do agree with his assessment regarding cohesiveness. But cohesiveness comes with compromise. What is lacking is a general concern to meet in the middle, to meet half-way, to find common ground on hot button issues, to find a place in which both Democrats and Republicans can come together for the greater good. Sadly, what has happened and continued to be exposed like a rotting tooth was the actuality of the fact that two sides simply cannot seem to agree on anything short of the fact that the sky is blue(ish). Even with something as simple agreeing on the color of the sky Trump himself worked carefully to skew the vision of a number of people that have decided that the sky is perhaps purple or pink by way of touting unfounded conspiracy theories. This decline became clearer during these past four years under the Trump Administration. I believe that Trump is not as unintelligent as some may believe. He saw American Political system's slip showing and managed to put his hand right up her skirt and give it a tug. Now the political system itself became exposed.

Lastly, Fiorina makes the case about the decline by stating it's weaknesses. For example, Fiorina asserts that "the weakening of party has contributed directly to the severity of several of the important problems the nation faces" such as "immobilism, single issue politics and popular alienation from government" all of which are symptoms of a sickness that is not so mysteriously rooted in financial gain and control. This is how Trump succeeded and how he continues to stoke the fires of various politicians to remaining loyal to him, not to the party itself. It is clear that even the Republican party has been hijacked and is beginning to split within itself. In essence, for the first time potentially, the Republican party is experiencing an identity crisis, of political views and ideologies. Reading further along, Nicole Rae, in his essay "Be Careful What You Wish For: The Rise of Responsible Parties in American National Politics" in The Enduring Debate, argues that "the parties have increasingly become defined by interests that attach themselves to one party or the other rather than truly straddling the two parties." What's more, Rae asserts that "the parties, in turn, must become more vigilant in defending those interests that attach to them, leaving little room to work with members of the other party to solve problems." Rae has punctuated my previous point pertaining to our Democracy and our decline, being the result of corporate interests, which also directly alters the mood concerning party affiliations, especially by those who, for one reason or another, do not see the "system" working for them, rather they experience the system working against them.

Essay #7

"U.S. House Members and Their Constituencies: An Exploration"

By Richard F. Fenno, Jr.

The essay by Richard F. Fenno, Jr. offers an insightful glimpse into the realities of Congressional Members and their constituencies, of which I will reference as "The Four Concentric Circles of Constituencies" in which Fenno has described in his essay, as the layers of constituencies representing four concentric circles, of which he explains in more depth. However, to better summarize the essay "U.S. House Members in Their Constituencies: An Exploration" I find it helpful to comb through what Fenno discusses regarding what these four concentric circles are and what they mean both in Washington as Fenno highlights and everywhere else. The distinction is made between Washington and the rest of the country because Fenno makes this distinction known as he explores the constituencies and House Members. Washington, in many ways, based on the reading, is its own entity, separate from the rest of the country on many levels, with its own realm of reality, one that does not exactly resemble the realities of the commoner–the average citizen–everyday individual. Moreover, Fenno, based on this distinction, offers a kind of insight that is unique and engaging, one that allows the reader–the common person–the average citizen to gain a better understanding as to why constituencies hold so much value on the political stage both in Washington and in the rest of the country, particularly in the districts in which House Members hail from and are elected.

For example, when we think of "constituencies" we all tend to, more often than not, think of simply, "voters". Perhaps some of us more avid political participants, understand constituents as "voters" from the district in which a House Member was elected. Admittedly, prior to reading this essay, my understanding of what constituency meant was limited. That said, here is what Fenno asserts regarding constituencies, their purpose, and their relevance. Imagine four circles, starting with an outer ring, followed by a smaller inner ring, followed by another smaller inner ring and finally a smaller ring at the center. Each ring represents a constituency. For instance, the first outer ring or concentric circle, represents "The Geographic Constituency" which represents the entire district. According to Fenno, "The District: The Geographic Constituency" is "the largest of these circles" which "represents the congressman's broadest view of his constituency." What's more, Fenno states that "it is the entity to which, from which, and in which he travels." Next there is the second inner ring and concentric circle, which represents "The Supporters: The Re-election Constituency". I consider this ring to include what I refer to as "super fans", "fans" and "necessary non-fans". These are the people who collectively elected a representative to represent "them" in their district. These individuals could include both Republicans and Democrats. Furthermore, the third inner ring, growing closer to the core of the U.S. House Member, within what Fenno calls "the nest of concentric circles", "The Strongest Supporters: The Primary Constituency". I call these individuals "super fans". These individuals are people who, as Fenno describes as those supporters who support a House Member "regardless of who the challenger may be." Moreover, "within each re-election constituency are nested these "others"–a constituency perceived as "my strongest supporters," "my hardcore support," "my loyalists," "my true believers," "my political base."

Finally, there is the fourth inner-most ring, the "inner sanctum" as I consider it to be. This inner-most, concentric circle, is regarded as "The Intimates: The Personal Constituency". According to Fenno, this inner circle within the primary constituency, are "the few individuals whose relationship with him is so personal and so intimate that their relevance to him cannot be captured by their inclusion in any description of "very strongest supporters." Additionally, "in some cases they are his closest political advisers and confidants. In other cases, they are people from whom he draws emotional sustenance for his political work." Fenno suggests that we should "think of these people as his personal constituency." Fenno highlights this circle, this "personal constituency" as "the most idiosyncratic of the several constituencies. This is the circle of "intimates" who are closest to the House Member, who more often than not, get to see this individual in rare form. Whereas the rest of the world does not, perhaps not even Washington. This inner sanctum is the core of the Congressional Member. The core of any element is typically the strongest, the most resilient, the most durable in a manner of speaking. This understanding became known to Fenno. For example, Fenno states that "in sum, my impression is that House members perceive four constituencies–geographical, re-election, primary, and personal–each one nesting within the previous one." This nest is an important nest, a nest in which House Members work to maintain by visiting home and maintaining close connections and ties with others form their hometown or district. This back and forth between home and Washington has its limits as Fenno has stated, has created tension and frustration for House Members as their legislative workload increases.

In short, Fenno states "it is harder to sustain a genuine two-way relationship–of a policy or an extra-policy sort–than it once was." These two realities are the "home relationship" and "Congress's institutional" responsibilities, both of which are hard to balance.

Essay #8

Social change and the pursuit of justice

Martin Luther King Jr. and Abraham Lincoln both have worked tirelessly in pursuit of social change and social justice over the course of their lifetime until their untimely death by way of assassination. Though one a lawyer, state representative and eventually president and the other a pastor, civil rights leader and activist, both played key roles in changing the laws of the land which greatly affected African American's in this country. Both succeeded at changing laws which kept black people in chains on a plantation somewhere and later kept black people separated from white people in segregationist states. Though there is about a 126 years between the two regarding their speeches, each labored to inspire change and raise awareness to the myriad of injustices against black people and anyone who sought to assist them in their cause for freedom and liberty, such as abolitionists, sympathizers, freedom riders, protestors, church goers, bus drivers, patrons, other politicians who's cause aligned with both men and more. All of this being said, both the Letter from Birmingham in 1963 and the Lyceum Address in 1838 focused on the issues which have been a plague in this country and that is racial discrimination in the forms of enslavement, slavery, police brutality, mob brutality, segregation, suppression, oppression, humiliation, abuse and murder of black people living in predominantly southern states, including some members of society who are in favor of so-called law and order, which more often than not included unfair, unjust and inhumane treatment of black people and anyone else who sided with them.

The similarities between these two speeches are clear. Both seek to bring the previously mentioned issues to light and to raise the awareness of acts committed by those who seek to unjustly cause harm and oppress black people outrightly. Both speeches underscore the importance of action in changing the laws of the land, uphold the constitutional rights of black people as citizens of this country and illustrate the necessity for federal government to act accordingly and swiftly. For example, Lincoln passionately states that "the operation of this mobocratic spirit, which all must admit, is now abroad in the land, the strongest bulwark of any Government, and particularly of those constituted like ours, may effectually be broken down and destroyed--I mean the attachment of the People." Lincoln continues to state the opposite effect if action is not taken. For instance, Lincoln claims that "whenever this effect shall be produced among us; whenever the vicious portion of population shall be permitted to gather in bands of hundreds and thousands, and burn churches, ravage and rob provision-stores, throw printing presses into rivers, shoot editors, and hang and burn obnoxious persons at pleasure, and with impunity; depend on it, this Government cannot last."

Lincoln's call to action at age twenty-eight as a State Representative and Lawyer at the time was to let anyone who is willing to hear, to understand that justice for all is exactly that. That justice and the pursuit of liberty and peace are not restricted to only some members of this great country but extend to all citizens, male and female, black and white, poor and rich, merchant and farmer. Similarly, Martin Luther King Jr. expressed his moral imperative to do the work and to act for the betterment of all black people, not just some black people. King's position, however, was specifically addressing the subjugation of black

American's in general through signs and lines, and seating areas keeping black people here or there, as well as the overall poor treatment black people in public spaces, in shops, diners, or any other business in which white people did not wish to have black people enter. King's position dialed in abuse of authority by the police and their brutality against black people. For example, King asserts in The Letter from Birmginham Jail, "injustice anywhere is a threat to justice everywhere. We are caught in an inescapable network of mutuality, tied in a single garment of destiny. Whatever affects one directly, affects all indirectly." King continues to punctuate his point with the poignant realties writing to his fellow clergymen that "Birmingham is probably the most thoroughly segregated city in the United States. Its ugly record of police brutality is known in every section of the country. Its unjust treatment of Negroes in the courts is a notorious reality. There have been more unsolved bombings of Negro homes and churches in Birmingham than in any city in this nation. These are the hard, brutal, and unbelievable facts."

The only real differences between these two speeches are one, King was in the middle of a peace protest who happened to be jailed for his actions. King's letter was a letter to illustrate the need to act and take action and to not sit idly by in a state of complacency or in a state of rage and anger as he points out regarding the Nation of Islam, Elijah Muhammad and the Muslim movement. King's letter was a letter to make his position known and provided steps outlining the process in which he is engaged. Lincoln's letter was more about raising the awareness of what could happen if action is not taken regarding slavery and the enslaved, and regarding mob rule and those nefarious individuals who seek to oppress others and who have sprung "up among the pleasure hunting masters of Southern slaves, and the order loving citizens of the land of steady habits." Lincoln's very long address goes on and on sharing examples of injustice, murder and how the court has failed regarding black people. Perhaps Lincoln was in his own way protesting the evil of the land which he himself believed that if left unchecked would be the ruin of this country. Perhaps his letter to address fellow members of the Lyceum was a petition to the people who would listen and who would consider their positions regarding slavery, enslavement and ill-treatment of anyone who supports the freedom of all people. Perhaps Lincoln used his time at the Lyceum addressing the very real and disturbing concerns and criminal acts committed against those who seek peace, freedom, life, liberty and the pursuit of happiness. Perhaps Lincoln's speech was his own sermon on the mount so-to-speak to wake people up to the truths that evil condemnation is afoot.

Works Cited

Jr., Martin Luther King. "Letter from Birmingham Jail." 1963.
Lincoln, Abraham. "Lyceum Address." 1838.

Closing Thoughts

Firstly, I wish to express my gratitude for taking the time to read this book. It had been in progress for a few years. Not that it took me so long to write it, but that I have been in college since 2019 when I started this book and had recently graduated May 2024 from Temple University. In this time, I had grown in so many ways. And this book was written in the early stages of my academic journey and only recently completed. That being said, and knowing what I know now, I think this book reflects a host of perspectives and insights relating to the world of politics. And given where we are currently, with an upcoming 2024 election between Biden and Trump, the completion of this book seems timely. Additionally, I have, as of today, May 29, switched back to being an Independent voter, because the way things are on both sides of the political isle are woefully out of balance. Though I will need to vote for someone, I will be voting, not for that someone but for Democracy as I know it. I am not voting for a political figure head, but a system of politics that is rooted or suppose to be rooted in equality and justice for all. An autocracy is not an option for me. Hopefully, it is not for you either.

Sources

1. Legal Voting Age By Country. Worldatlas.com

2. Kazin, Michael. (2019) Awakening from the '60's Generation. Nymag.com

3. Alt-Right. Wikipedia

4. History of the Democratic and Republican Parties. U.S. Embassy

5. Ku Klux Klan: A history of Racism. (2011). www.splcenter.org

6. Black Americans in Congress. U.S. House.gov

7. Ginsberg, Lewis et al. We The People. pp. 213-217

8. Trumpism. Wikipedia

9. New Democrat. Wikipedia

10. Political Moderate. Wikipedia

11. About Us. U.S. House.gov

12. Moderate Republicans. Moderate Republicans.com

13. Rockefeller Republican. Wikipedia

14. Whig Party. Ohio History Central.org

15. Centrism. Wikipedia

16. Centrism. Encyclopedia.com

17. Psychosocial. APA Dictionary of Psychology

18. Construct. Oxford Languages

19. Horseshoe Theory. Rational Wiki

20. Berlatsky, Noah. Let's put an end to the horseshoe theory once and for all. Pacific Standard.

21. Muscato, Christopher. Criticism of the horseshoe theory. Study.com

22. Theory. Oxford Languages

23. Chen, James. Communism. Investopedia

24. Fascism. Wikipedia

25. O'Malley, J.P. Communism and Fascism: The Reason They Are So Similar. The Daily Beast

26. Weisberger, Wendy. What is Fascism? Live Science.com

27. Schneider, Howard. Trump is Right, Jobs for black Americans abound: Here's why it may not last. Reuters

28. Socialism. Investopedia

29. How Welfare began in the United States. Constitutional Rights Foundation.

30. Cares Act. Wikipedia

31. Conservatism. Britannica

32. Conservatism. Merriam-Webster Dictionary

33. Klein, Daniel B. (2014) The Origin of Liberalism. The Atlantic

34. Liberalism. Britannica

www.ingramcontent.com/pod-product-compliance
Lightning Source LLC
Chambersburg PA
CBHW072046280526
45788CB00006B/2203